South-East QUEENSLAND

A DISCOVERY GUIDE

Photography by Steve Parish

Text by Bob Johnson & Peter Fox

Rockhampton
Townsville
Meekay
Mackay

Steve Parish
PUBLISHING

www.steveparish.com.au

Contents

North of Brisbane   60–87

West of Brisbane   88–99

South of Brisbane   100–121

Introduction

South-East Queensland will always be a very special place for me – not only because of the wealth of inspiring natural beauty in the south-east corner, but also because the region has been my home and principal place of business for more than twenty years. I have travelled the length and breadth of this vast, beautiful land and although I could live happily in any of Australia's cities – and I have in many – Brisbane is the city that I am proud to call home. Here, working from my office in a sprawling Queenslander, is where I feel most at ease and where I am at my most inspired. It gives me no end of pleasure to share this wonderful region with others through my books and photographs.

When I first moved to Queensland, at the age of twenty-nine, I was captivated by the city's friendliness and its potential. Situated on the meandering loops of the Brisbane River, Brisbane is rated as one of the world's most liveable cities, and it certainly is! Its enviable climate gives it a laid-back charm, but I found that Brisbane also offered everything else I required from a city: efficient transport and administration, world-class theatres, galleries and cultural centres, excellent shopping, fine restaurants and tidy, safe suburban streets. I took up a job as a photographer with the Queensland Parks and Wildlife Service and it was then that the rich natural heritage of the city and its surrounds was revealed to me.

Close to the capital are charming heritage towns and flourishing cities, as well as beaches, lush national parks and rugged mountain ranges, all of which provide homes for the multitude of plants and animals that inhabit South-East Queensland. It was this spectacular display of nature's wonders that prompted me to find a way to share the beauty I saw through my lens with others, by starting my own fledgling publishing company. Locals embraced my business enthusiastically and I am forever indebted to Queenslanders for the encouragement, assistance and support I received.

In order to share this treasure-trove of natural and created attractions, I traversed the highways and byways, trekked through dense scrub and dived off the stunning South-East Queensland coast, uncovering the region's mysteries for myself – and I was delighted with what I found. If I wanted to escape the city to find solitude, serenity or solutions in the natural world, a short drive led me to massive lakes, World-Heritage-listed rainforests or seemingly endless, nearly secluded beaches. If I wanted to photograph the unique character of Australia and Australians, I could easily visit one of the many sprawling, welcoming country towns. Despite my familiarity with South-East Queensland, whenever I come to do a new book on the region I am astonished anew at just how much this area has to offer. There is so much to discover, so many new adventures to be had in South-East Queensland that, even after twenty years of being a "local", I am still excited to get behind the wheel of my car for a driving tour.

Whether you intend to use this guide to enliven your weekends, or whether you wish to embark on a longer driving tour of South-East Queensland, I hope that, when you open this book and get a glimpse of what awaits, you feel the same joyful anticipation that I feel on my frequent trips around the region – the knowledge that your exploration will reveal a truly magnificent and unique part of Australia.

Left: Steve has explored South-East Queensland for over 20 years. *Right:* The region is renowned for its excellent surf and swimming beaches.

How to Use this Book

This book has been designed with all readers in mind, whether domestic daytrippers wanting to explore – or escape – the city, or international travellers planning a more extensive tour around the South-East Queensland region. Whatever your objective, simple-to-follow maps, tried-and-tested driving tours, interesting snippets of local and natural history, and lists of "Things to See and Do" presented in stand-out sidebars, make this book one of the most straightforward guides to what you can expect to see on your travels throughout the South-East. Our local authors have covered almost every kilometre of this vast region, so you can be sure that this guide recommends the best that it has to offer. Marvel at the scenic and wildlife wonders or enjoy the towns and built attractions, but, above all, enjoy your stay!

Region-by-Region Format

In order to showcase the sheer diversity of adventures packed into Queensland's South-East corner, this guide is split into five sections with the pages throughout colour-coded by region. Each section contains a full-page map on which the major towns, attractions, national parks and driving tours along highways and byways are indicated. In each of the five regions – Brisbane city, Brisbane Surrounds, North of Brisbane, West of Brisbane, South of Brisbane – you'll be introduced to the area's history, geography and major industries. Also covered are national parks and flora and fauna, as well as the region's cultural and ecological significance.

The region-by-region format leads from the modern metropolis of Brisbane to the surrounding greenery, heritage towns and numerous attractions of Moreton Bay to the east. North and south lie the pristine beaches and cosmopolitan glamour of the Gold and Sunshine Coasts. To the West tower the rugged mountains of the Great Dividing Range and some of Australia's most prized grazing and farming land. Of course, rather than being distinct entities, these regions overlap and merge, so, wherever possible, the driving tours and maps within this guide venture into the boundaries of adjoining regions to explain the easiest way to travel from one area of South-East Queensland to the next.

Natural History Break-out Boxes

South-East Queensland's diverse habitats protect a multitude of plant and animal life. Bays, lakes, rainforests and national parks teem with flora and fauna of all description, but even the cities, suburbs and towns are home to possums, birds and reptiles that the keen-eyed visitor can hope to see. Eye-catching break-out boxes scattered throughout explain the natural history of the area and give you a sneak preview of the species you can expect to see and where best to see them.

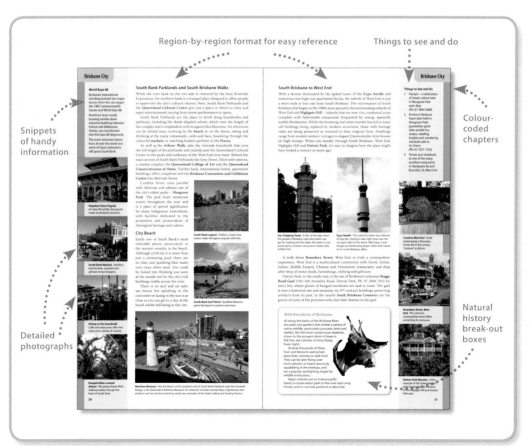

Location, Location, Location

For your convenience, the location and contact details of rangers' stations, tourist attractions and advisory bodies are listed in the text in each chapter or in the "Things to See and Do" column on the relevant spread.

How to Use the Maps

Consistent, easy-to-read maps walk you through the major attractions and best tours for each section. Use the map in each chapter to locate the attractions, which are explained at length – giving address and contact details – in the text. Maps have been designed to show all of the major attractions mentioned.

Popular bushwalking and hiking trails, camping grounds and scenic driving tours are mentioned in detail in the text, providing you with numerous options for "going bush".

Things to See and Do

Each State of Australia has its own flavour and offers a number of natural and created surprises. Listed in this section of all Steve Parish Guides are the top "must-see" activities for travellers wanting to make the most of their trip.

Whether you want to enjoy a heritage tour of historic houses or you'd prefer to visit bustling markets, colourful festivals, thrilling theme parks or wildlife sanctuaries, this section gives you the low-down on the area's not-to-be-missed attractions. You'll even discover where to stop on the roadside to get the best views of the region's landscape.

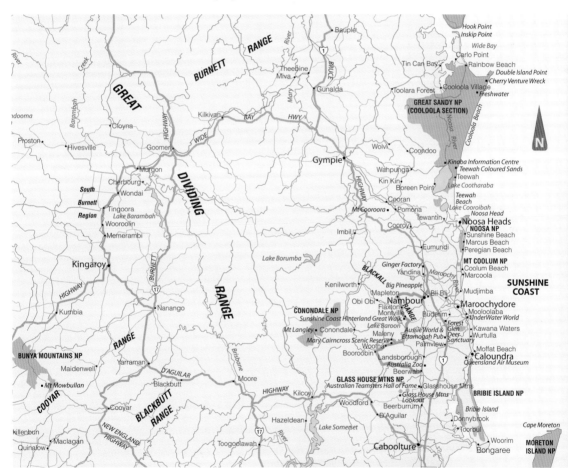

Dramatic Driving Tours

Australia is a vast continent, and yet at almost every twist and turn of the road South-East Queensland offers something new to see from your car window. This guide takes you on a driving tour from the city to the unique splendour of Fraser Island, following the most spectacularly scenic routes. Use the instructive text, with the maps as back-up, to wind your way over the region's highways and byways, stopping at the best lookouts, picnic areas, tourist sites, nature reserves and historic sites, all via the region's most charming towns.

The Big Picture

Queensland is Australia's second-largest State and one of the nation's most diverse and most celebrated. It is home to over four million people, many of whom choose to reside in the State's spectacularly sunny, attraction-packed south-east corner. "Beautiful one day, perfect the next", is the motto, but that doesn't detail the sheer degree of natural perfection attained in this compact area filled with emerald rainforest, shimmering lakes, imposing mountains, snow-white beaches and rolling fields of wheat and sugar cane.

Sugar cane farming began at Moreton Bay in 1864, and sugar soon became a major industry.

The region's popularity is not due to its natural beauty alone: its absorbing history is preserved in many historic sites and buildings, and its cities and regional centres are respectively stylish and modern or charmingly quaint. Add bountiful wildlife, friendly locals, and tourist attractions and it's easy to see why the area is one of Australia's fastest-growing holiday destinations.

By the turn of the 20th century, Brisbane was a busy, wealthy capital with a bright future.

Colonisation to Settlement

As one of the last States to be settled, Queensland soon made up for being a late bloomer with a population boom in the late 1850s that saw the wealth and status of the fledgling colony rapidly increase.

The Goldrushes of the 1860s and 70s saw settlers flock to Gympie (*above*) and other gold towns.

The local Indigenous people, who had enjoyed the mild climate and abundant wildlife for centuries, were described by Flinders at the time of exploration as friendly, but, with the establishment of a penal colony in 1824 and then a free settlement in 1840, they were relocated to make way for the development of Brisbane and the agricultural heartlands of the Darling Downs.

Agriculture to Industry

The State's early growth rode on the back of pastoral pursuits. In 1859, just twelve cows were recorded in the colony; by 1870 there were a million – and eight million sheep. Grazing and sugar-cane farming required cleared land, which fed the timber industry and allowed for the construction of buildings and businesses, especially by those who profited in the goldrushes of the 1860s. In 1865, railway tracks – the harbingers of industry – were built.

Qld Rail, with a home base in Ipswich, opened up the State from 1865 onwards.

Access to port facilities, on the Brisbane River and elsewhere, was imperative for Qld's growth.

The Effect of Settlement on Aborigines and Wildlife

Unfortunately for Queensland's native animals and Indigenous inhabitants, early European settlers did little to conserve culture or the environment.

Aborigines were, at best, ignored or treated as unpaid slave labour on the large sheep and cattle stations that saw the boom of the State's agricultural industry. At worst, they were massacred in reprisal for protecting their territory. Settlers also paid little heed to the environmental degradation caused by clearing land, overgrazing and the trampling feet of introduced stock.

20th Century to Present

On the first day of the 20th century, Queensland entered the modern era with a vote to join the other States to become part of the Commonwealth of Australia. However national unity did not diminish earlier loyalties and many thousands of Queenslanders still enlisted to fight for England in the Boer War and World War I. The peacetime that followed World War II ushered in a decade of repopulation and the relaxation of previously strict migration policies, which created today's multicultural Queensland. In tune with this period of ethnic diversification was Expo 88, the 1988 celebration of culture from around the world, which put Brisbane on the world stage and led to further growth and development in the 1990s.

Expo 88 led to the establishment of the leisure precinct of South Bank on the former Expo site. Many buildings, sculptures and exhibits from Expo 88, such as this café above and the Nepalese temple at South Bank, are dotted around the city.

A Brief History of Queensland

1770 – Captain James Cook first landed in Qld.

1824 – A penal colony was established at Moreton Bay and became notorious for its harsh treatment of prisoners.

1840 – The first free settler arrived near Ipswich.

1842 – The entire Moreton Bay area was opened up for settlement. Ipswich was established.

1859 – The colony of Queensland was established and the *Qld Unoccupied Crown Lands Occupation Act* brought an influx of settlers.

Below, top to bottom: **Main Beach on the Gold Coast; Fraser Island.**

Delights for the Visitor

South-East Queensland today is a premier holiday destination with surf, sand, sun and pockets of wilderness, such as the World-Heritage-listed Central Eastern Rainforest Reserves, unmatched by any in the world. Inland, its country charm is unmistakable. For thrillseekers, the glamorous Gold Coast with its many theme parks is not to be missed. Whatever your tastes, South-East Queensland promises – and provides.

Geology, Topography and Climate in the South-East

Over 55 million years ago, when the giant southern supercontinent of Gondwana began its slow separation, what is now the continent of Australia was covered in temperate rainforest. Although pockets of rainforest remain in Queensland's north and south-east corner, as Australia drifted away from Antartica and became more arid, its climate, topography and native flora and fauna changed.

The molten red core of the earth threw up rocky ridges and active volcanoes that dramatically altered the landscape. Slowly the continent's surfaces were eroded and the heat favoured drought-resistant eucalypts, low lying scrub, acacias, and Australia's hardy marsupial mammals and reptiles.

To say that the geology and climate are varied is an understatement. While much of the South-East Queensland region is typified by its near year-round sunshine, it is also a region quite used to unexpected squalls, droughts, floods and even cyclones. By the coast, the sweltering heat is often cooled by Pacific Ocean breezes or the downpours that follow bruising, sky-rending thunderstorms in summer. Inland, to the west and in the higher-altitude granite belt, seasons are more obvious: crackling winter frosts being replaced by parched summers. In the central eastern rainforest, the humidity rises. To the north, on the Sunshine Coast or Fraser Island, and even in Brisbane itself, there are really only two seasons: summer and a month or so of cooler weather that constitutes winter. Sunlovers can expect the temperature to hover between 20 and 30° Celsius, give or take 5°, for most of the year.

Droughts and Flooding Rains

South-East Queensland, like much of Australia, is subject to extremes. Over the centuries the landscape has been scarred by drought and scored by torrents flowing from flooded creeks and rivers. Drought is a near-annual threat in the Western Downs. It seems that in the south-east corner the old adage "it never rains, it pours" is certainly true. Brisbane city has been inundated by floodwaters over eight times, with the worst in 1974. Throughout 1863 much of South-East Queensland experienced unseasonable flooding and in 1983 all of Queensland was declared a disaster area following floods.

Lamington National Park

Traces of Australia's warmer, wetter days are embodied by the lush rainforest preserved in the Central Eastern Rainforest Reserves at Lamington National Park. Here, moss and tree ferns trail over buttress roots that crisscross the forest floor.

Edward Street during the 1974 floods

Many of Brisbane city's buildings were awash with debris following the floods of 1974. Twelve people lost their lives to the waters and the city recorded its highest ever floodwater level. A flood marker in the City Botanic Gardens shows the high water mark.

Victoria Point, Moreton Bay

The blue expanse of Moreton Bay lends a cool sea change to the city and coast, but often conjures up dramatic storms.

Brisbane Valley

Graziers despair and pray for rain over the drier months of winter in the Brisbane and Lockyer valleys and further west in the wheat belt.

Rugged Mountain Ranges

Underpinning the scenic beauty of South-East Queensland are the towering peaks and rocky shelves that make up the backbone of the State. Rugged mountain ranges embrace the region to the south, north and west. The hills and dales of the coastal hinterland were formed by fiery volcanic eruptions that occurred millions of years ago in the mountains of the Scenic Rim and McPherson Ranges to the south and the Glass House Mountains to the north. Now, the surrounding, gently undulating land punctuated with spent volcanic plugs is blessed with rich soil that nourishes South-East Queensland's fruit- growing industry. To the west, running parallel with much of Queensland's 5208-km coastline, is the Great Dividing Range, which stretches from the northeastern tip of Queensland down through New South Wales to the Grampians in western Victoria. The craggy Main Range section of the Great Dividing Range separates the flat, fertile plains of the Darling Downs from the wallam heath, casuarina and banksia scrub of the coastal region.

The Beautiful East Coast

Stretching along the east coast are the sparkling blue, white-capped waters of the Pacific Ocean, which flow into the expanse of water known as Moreton Bay. The bay creates a natural harbour around the mouth of the Brisbane River and is remarkable thanks to its unusual formation. A string of giant sand islands buffer the mainlaind from the ocean swells to create the Bay. Underneath these sand giants, an equally large deposit of sand has created a shelf on the ocean floor and the foundations of Moreton Island, North and South Stradbroke Islands and Fraser Island lie on this ledge. But these sand-covered islands are far from desert; their massive dunes are covered with forests, heaths and swamps that support diverse ecosystems and wildlife, some species remaining significantly unaffected by evolutionary changes to mainland relatives.

In the water, marine life enjoys the temperate ocean, secluded beaches and mangrove-fringed estuaries that create safe egg-laying sites for turtles and certain species of fish. Further out, in the depths beyond the breakers, Humpback, Sperm and Southern Right Whales frolic and make migratory journeys along the coastline. Coral reefs colour the seabed, protecting reef fish and invertebrates, while the islands of the Bay, many unpopulated, are a haven for seabirds and migratory waders.

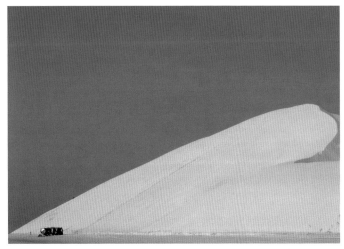 

Fraser Island

The unique environment of Fraser Island makes it a treasure not only for its creature occupants, but for the world. It is the largest sand island on earth and supports woodland and habitat that shelters hundreds of species of wildlife, even some that are rare and endangered.

Moreton Island

Mountains of snow-white sand delight visitors to Moreton Island, who can enjoy the fun of sand-tobogganing down the steep slopes.

Paniyiri Dancers add a touch of the Aegean to Musgrave Park during the Greek festival.

Queensland's world-class art galleries house a collection of admired works.

The Dragon Boat Race is a popular competition during River Festival.

Australia Day Parade Riders remember Australia's bushranging days by donning Ned Kelly-style armour.

Culture and Celebration

Once considered the country cousin to the more artistically and culturally mature southern States, Queensland's rapid growth has seen it transformed into a multicultural, dynamic and creative State. Residents of South-East Queensland enjoy acclaimed performances of theatre, ballet, opera and modern dance at the **Queensland Performing Arts Complex**. They muse over exhibits of modern art or reminisce over classics at the **Queensland Art Gallery**, and they wonder at displays about the continent's prehistory on show at the **Queensland Museum**. On top of this, they throng to annual events, be it to celebrate Australia Day, Anzac Day, cultural heritage or festivals of the arts.

In the Cities

Each New Year's Eve, Brisbane city is lit with colourful fireworks displays to farewell the old year and usher in the new. But throughout the year Brisbane and the cities of the south-east corner host many celebrations. January 26 is the annual **Australia Day** holiday and street parade. In March and April, the **Streets of Brisbane** festival at South Bank includes various street performances. Caxton Street's annual **Seafood and Wine Festival** vies for calendar space with the **Queensland Jazz Carnival**, **Queensland Winter Racing Carnival**, and **Paniyiri** festival each May. In June, Musgrave Park takes a step back in time with the **Medieval Fayre**, when knights and jesters, wandering minstrels and damsels enliven the park. August and September see the **Brisbane International Film Festival**, the **Brisbane Festival**, the **Spring Hill Fair** and the **September Moon Festival** in Chinatown, while October draws the literary set to the **Brisbane Writers' Festival**. Throughout the south-east, towns and cities host a range of enticing events, from the **King of the Mountain Festival** in Pomona each July to **Gympie Country Music Muster** in August, **Esk Multicultural Festival** in September, and the **Woodford Folk Festival** from 27 December to 1 January each year.

On the Rivers, Lakes, Bays and Beaches

Yacht races, kite flying competitions and fishing competitions are all to be found year-round on the many beaches that grace South-East Queensland. Brisbane city pays homage to the Brisbane River each September with the week-long **River Festival**, featuring the spectacular fireworks display of River*fire* and many water-themed events. The following month, the State's largest fishing competition, the **Kirkleigh Klassic**, attracts thousands of keen anglers to nearby Lake Somerset to try their luck at catching Bass, Yellowbelly, Silver Perch and Eel-tailed Catfish.

The Ekka

Sample bags, roaring and rattling rides, dagwood dogs, the menagerie of the grand parade and the thrills of Sideshow Alley – the Royal Brisbane Exhibition, fondly known as the Ekka, is an annual event not to be missed. It takes place each August at the RNA Exhibition Grounds to the city's north-east and is a ten-day spectacular important enough to warrant a public holiday known as "People's Day". Agricultural produce and livestock, flowers, homemade cakes, jams and furnishings are displayed and judged. Rural competitions, such as woodchopping, are held and the winners much lauded. Each year, the Ekka's carnival atmosphere and showbiz hustle and bustle draw ever-increasing crowds (Ph: 07 3852 1831 for details).

Coolum's annual **Kite Festival** in September is a pleasant seaside excursion for families. In August, the **Hervey Bay Whale Festival** is a carnival to honour the return of the migratory behemoths to the Sunshine Coast. Excellent sailing conditions along the coast attract enthusiasts from near and far to the **Sydney–Mooloolaba Yacht Race** and **Brisbane–Gladstone Yacht Race**, both held in April, and the **Bay to Bay Yacht Race** from Tin Can Bay to Hervey Bay in May.

In Moreton Bay, North Stradbroke Island holds the **Point Lookout Inshore Rescue Boat Classic Carnival** on the last weekend in May and the **Straddie Assault** surfing event in October. The Gold Coast is the destination for yacht races as well as host to the **Australian Surf Lifesaving Championships**.

Above: Kids love the colourful fun of Coolum's annual Kite Festival.

Below: Brisbane city is illuminated by a spectacular pyrotechnic display each September when the city celebrates River*fire*. The week-long River Festival includes a range of events, but the fireworks are the most eagerly anticipated.

Bottom right: The Carnival of Flowers showcases the floral beauty of Toowoomba, which is known as the "Garden City".

Further Information

1 **Brisbane Tourism**, City Hall, King George Sq, Brisbane (Ph: 07 3221 8411)

2 **Toowoomba & Golden West Tourist Association** 4 Little St, Toowoomba (Ph: 07 4623 1988)

3 **Tourism Sunshine Coast**, Cnr River Esp. & Parkyn Parade, Mooloolaba (Ph: 07 5477 7311)

4 **Fraser Coast South Burnett Tourism Board,** 3844 Kent St, Maryborough (Ph: 07 4122 3444)

5 **Gold Coast Tourism Bureau**, 2nd Fl, 64 Ferny Ave, Surfers Paradise (Ph: 07 5592 2699)

Floral Festivities

Toowoomba blooms in September with the annual Carnival of Flowers, but not to be outdone are Warwick – with its Annual Autumn Flower Show in March, Allora in the far south-east with the Allora Sunflower Festival, or Mt Tamborine with the August Flower and Garden Festival. Also revelling in all things floral is Maleny in the Sunshine Coast Hinterland, which holds the Festival of Colour in November.

Brisbane City

Brisbane, Australia's third-largest city, is a vibrant, subtropical metropolis that has long shrugged off any "big country town" criticism. Geography and climate have largely dictated the city's laid-back character, with year-round sunshine and the wide, winding Brisbane River creating a relaxing lifestyle for locals. In days past, the river divided the city, but today's main thoroughfares radiate from the city centre, in Queen Street, over the many bridges to the outer suburbs. Many of these routes follow the old wagon trails that plotted the easiest path beside the river or along the scrub-covered ridges.

Crimson Rosella

Brisbane's suburban sprawl is home to over one and a half million people, yet it is not so big that there are cities within the city. When you walk through the city centre or across the Victoria or Goodwill bridges to South Bank, or take a ferry ride around the city reaches, you can feel the well-defined shape and size of the city's heart.

From Convict Post to Vibrant Capital

For thousands of years, Indigenous people lived and hunted among the rivers, creeks, rainforests and hills where the city of Brisbane now stands. In 1823, European exploration began with John Oxley discovering the Brisbane River, where he stopped for fresh water at a site mid-way along North Quay. The following year, British colonists established the Moreton Bay convict settlement, first at Redcliffe and then where the city-centre skyscrapers stand today, and so began the influx of European culture.

When the Governor of New South Wales, Sir Thomas Brisbane, visited the Redcliffe settlement in December 1824, he was taken to inspect the area where John Oxley had landed. The name Brisbane was chosen for the site, but it was often called Moreton Bay until 1839 when it ceased to be a penal colony and the name Brisbane came into common use. In 1859, the Colony of Queensland separated from New South Wales and Brisbane became its capital. In 1901, when the Australian colonies formed the Commonwealth of Australia, Brisbane became capital of the State of Queensland.

Brisbane Today

Modern Brisbane is a vibrant city with a mix of heritage buildings from the 19th and 20th centuries and world-class social, educational, cultural and sporting facilities to take it forward in the 21st century – during which, like most Australian capitals, it is expected to continue to flourish.

Top to bottom: **St Helena convict jail ruins; Queenslander-style architecture; Alice Street high-rise; Tropical Dome, Brisbane Botanic Gardens, Mt Coot-tha.**

Riverside Centre from Kangaroo Point at dawn The Riverside Centre is abuzz with restaurants and entertainment among the high-rise business and commercial buildings of the Eagle Street precinct. It is also a starting point for paddlewheeler river cruises.

Getting Around

Central Brisbane is easy to travel around by car, bus, rail, ferry, bicycle or on foot. **Bus services** run throughout the city and suburbs, including special loop routes in the city centre. **Suburban trains** from the north, south-west, south and east converge through stations at **South Brisbane**, **Roma Street** (the intrastate and interstate transit centre), **Central**, and **Brunswick Street** in Fortitude Valley. Ferries, including the fast **CityCats**, ply the river. Train, bus and ferry services also have a common ticketing system, making it cheaper and easier for visitors to travel around the city on a day pass. For those who prefer to cycle, many winding bike paths circle through the city's parks and suburbs.

Above, top to bottom: Cycle or walk over the Goodwill Bridge between South Bank and Gardens Point; CityCat ferries provide fast river transport.

Further Information

Brisbane Tourism Information Centres
Queen St Mall
(Ph: 07 3229 5918)

City Hall, King George Sq
(Ph: 07 3221 8411)

Brisbane City Council Call Centre
(Ph: 07 3403 8888)

Naturally Queensland Information Centre/EPA
Ground Flr, 160 Ann St Brisbane
(Ph: 07 3227 8187)

Trans Info – for public transport information
(Ph: 07 131 230)

Queensland Government Travel Centre
243 Edward St, Brisbane
(Ph: 07 3874 2800)

Clockwise from top left: **Goodwill Bridge; Story Bridge; William Jolly Bridge; Victoria Bridge**
The winding Brisbane River and the bridges that span it create pleasant vistas that can be enjoyed from the many riverside vantage points, from aboard the ferries or on the bridges themselves. The Goodwill Bridge is open only to pedestrians and cyclists. Other bridges, except the Captain Cook Bridge, have walkways. *Below right:* Treasury Casino and the Riverside Expressway, seen from South Bank.

You can **cycle** or **walk** the whole length of South Bank and down past the Queensland Cultural Centre, which houses the Performing Arts Complex, Queensland Art Gallery, the Museum and the State Library. From the southern end of South Bank Parklands, you can cross the pedestrian–cycle Goodwill Bridge, and enjoy lovely views upriver past the Victoria Bridge and down river past the Captain Cook Bridge and Kangaroo Point Cliffs, to the City Botanic Gardens.

Guides to heritage buildings and other interesting places within walking distance are available from the information centres in the Queen Street Mall and at South Bank.

City and River
The picture below shows the city centre's high-rise buildings behind the green, mangrove-fringed expanse of the City Botanic Gardens.

At the centre of the picture are the older skyscrapers that transformed the city skyline in the 1970s and 1980s, before which the City Hall tower was the tallest structure.

Towards the right are the buildings around the Riverside Centre, the financial and business hub. Further right, recent apartment buildings cluster near the northern end of the Story Bridge.

The CBD and Kangaroo Point

Brisbane's central business district is flanked to the south by the broad reaches of the Brisbane River and the red-gold cliffs of Kangaroo Point, a favoured recreational area between South Bank and the Story Bridge.

A Compact City

Early Brisbane grew from a settlement on the northern bank to include South Brisbane, which became the port, and Kangaroo Point. Today these three central areas are linked by four road bridges – the Story, Captain Cook, Victoria and William Jolly – as well as the pedestrian–cycle Goodwill Bridge and the Merivale Rail Bridge. Behind the giant loop of the river around Gardens Point is a cross-hatch of city streets – eight east-west streets named after queens of England (Ann, Adelaide, Queen, Elizabeth, Charlotte, Mary, Margaret and Alice) and four north-south named after kings (William, George, Albert and Edward). These streets, plus Turbot, Creek and Eagle Streets, make up the compact government, business and retail area, with Brisbane City Hall and King George Square at its centre.

1. Captain Cook Bridge 2. Mount Coot-tha 3. Queensland University of Technology
4. City Botanic Gardens 5. Riverside Centre 6. Story Bridge 7. Kangaroo Point

The Story of the Story Bridge

The Story Bridge links the city centre with Kangaroo Point and is Brisbane's largest structure. The 281-m cantilever truss steel bridge was designed by Dr J.C.C. Bradfield and opened in 1940. It was named after John Story, former vice-chancellor of the University of Queensland. At its highest point the bridge is almost 80 m above the river and people on the **Story Bridge Adventure Climb** (Ph: 07 3514 6900) have spectacular 360-degree views of the city, river, distant mountains and Moreton Bay.

Queen, Adelaide and Elizabeth Streets make up the city's shopping hub, while Edward and Albert Streets contain busy restaurants, cafés and bars. George Street is the government precinct, with Parliament House at the Gardens end and government office buildings on both sides.

South Brisbane, once a river port as rough and tough as any in the 19th century, has been transformed from an industrial area into a modern cultural, business and residential precinct. It boasts the much-lauded South Bank Parklands on the site of World Expo 88, the Queensland Cultural Centre and the Brisbane Convention and Exhibition Centre.

Kangaroo Point

Jutting out in another great loop of the river is Kangaroo Point. In the early days of the settlement, the Point was the end of the road for traders and travellers, a place of rough pubs, meatworks and rowdy wharves. Today it is a prime riverside residential area boasting excellent views of the city centre. It is also a great place for a riverside stroll or a barbecue.

Left: **Kangaroo Point** The River Terrace walk follows the edge of the Kangaroo Point cliffs – a great place to watch the sun set over the river and a popular place for rock climbing.

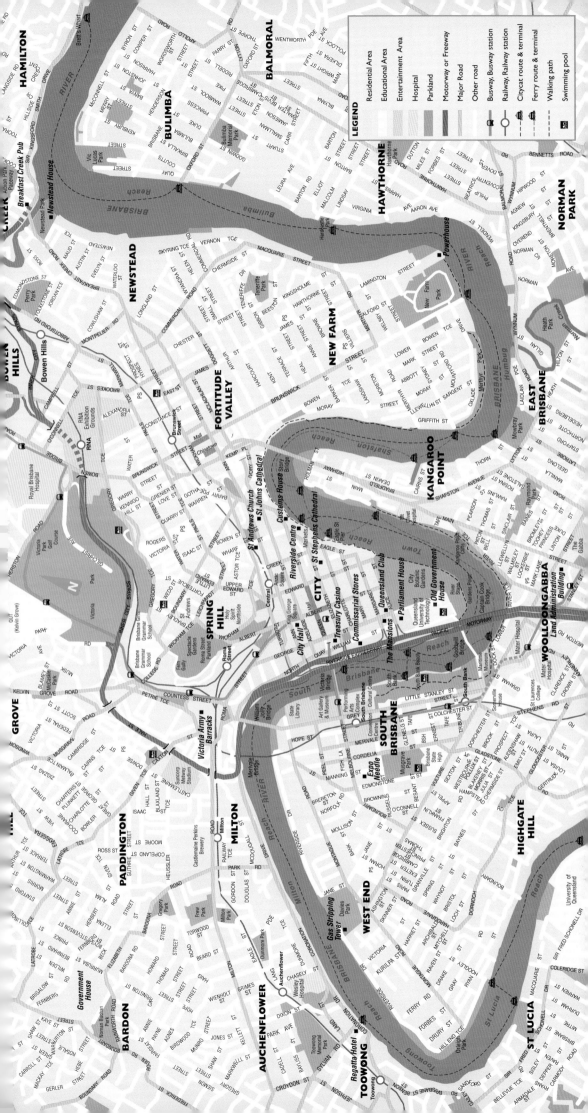

City of Contrasts

Brisbane is a city with two faces – an old face and a fresh, new look.

The old is gracious colonial-era sandstone buildings and ordered parks and gardens.

The new is brash, modern, tall steel and aluminium buildings with shining Gotham-City glass and tiles.

These two blend together in subtle juxtaposition to give a feeling of a solid heritage and an exciting future.

The Palace Hotel, Ann Street is a popular backpackers' hostel.

Parliament House, Alice Street

The old Land Administration Building, seen from Queens Park, is now the Conrad Hotel.

The Windmill, Wickham Terrace Brisbane's oldest building was built by convicts in 1828 and used to grind maize flour.

Brisbane City Hall and King George Square The Clock Tower has an observation deck.

Albert Street Uniting Church on the corner of Ann and Albert Streets.

A Walk Through Brisbane's Past

The only buildings to have survived Brisbane's convict days are **The Windmill** on Wickham Terrace and the **Commissariat Store** in William Street by the river. They were forerunners of dozens of buildings constructed between 1828 and the start of the high-rise era in the 1970s. Tall, new buildings now obscure even the **City Hall Clock Tower**, once the city's highest building. If you take the lift to the top of the Clock Tower, where you're surrounded by a forest of skyscrapers, imagine for a moment the cityscape without these modern buildings. You may just see the Brisbane of old – the buildings that comprise the city's architectural heritage.

To the south, at the far end of George, Albert and Edward Streets, you'll come to the green hemisphere of the **City Botanic Gardens**. At its right-hand edge you'll see the copper-domed **Parliament House**. This three-storey sandstone building, opened in 1869, dominates the Gardens end of the city. Beyond it is the two-storey sandstone **Old Government House**, where the State's first Governor, George Bowen, lived from its completion in 1862; the building is now home to the National Trust. Diagonally opposite Parliament House and overlooking the Gardens is the **Queensland Club**, a three-level Italianate Classic-Revival-style building from 1885.

Heading north along George Street, you will come to **The Mansions** (1890) on the corner of Margaret Street. This red-brick building – originally townhouses for Brisbane's wealthy – has been restored and is now offices. Next of the 19th-century survivors on your walk is the three-storey Gothic brick and sandstone **Government Printing Office** (1874). In 1883 it was the first building in Brisbane to have electric light. Between the old Printing Office and Queen Street stand two of the finest examples of colonial architecture: the **Land Administration Building** (1905), now the Conrad Hotel; and the **Treasury Building** (1885), now the Treasury Casino. **Queen's Park**, with a statue of Queen Victoria, lies between the two.

The Italian-Renaissance-style Treasury Building takes up the whole block bordered by Queen, George, Elizabeth and William Streets. It is restored externally to its original condition and restored internally within heritage guidelines.

Anzac Square, with the Shrine of Remembrance, is Brisbane's most significant war memorial.

Further along Queen Street from the Treasury Building is the retail heart of Brisbane, and just off the eastern end of the **Queen Street Mall** is the **Brisbane General Post Office**, dating from 1872. In front of the GPO is **Anzac Square**, containing the city's premier war memorial, the **Shrine of Remembrance** (1930), opposite which is **Central Station** (1901) in Ann Street. Behind the GPO you'll see **St Stephen's Cathedral** (1874) on Elizabeth Street, and beside that, **St Stephen's Church**, Brisbane's oldest, dating from 1850.

On the river bank further along Queen Street is **Customs House**, with its sandstone columns and copper dome dating from 1889. Today it is owned by the University of Queensland and is used as a reception and performance venue.

The Queensland Club in Alice Street overlooks the City Botanic Gardens.

Heritage Buildings

The Old Windmill
Comissariat Store
City Hall
Parliament House
Old Government House
Queensland Club
The Mansions
Government Printing Office
Land Administration Building
Treasury Building
General Post Office
St Stephen's Cathedral
Albert Street Uniting Church
St Andrew's Church
St John's Cathedral
St Paul's Church

Above, top to bottom: **Parliament House;** **The Mansions.** *Right:* **Customs House** on the river at the eastern end of Queen Street.

Also in this north-east quadrant of the city are four more historic churches. On the corner of Ann and Albert Streets is the pretty red brick, white-spired **Albert Street Uniting Church** (1889). Further to the east on Ann Street are **St Andrew's Church** (1905) and **St John's Cathedral** (1910), while the Spring Hill skyline is graced by **St Paul's Church** (1889).

Other City Attractions

The rewards for getting out and about in Brisbane are many. By day or night you'll find some entertainment or pastime to suit – galleries, theatres, dining, street entertainment, sporting events, nightclubbing, gaming, shopping, strolling in parks and gardens, river cruising or just sightseeing.

The city's bustling, vibrant centre is the **Queen Street Mall**. Once the main street, filled with cars, buses and, in earlier times, trams, today it is a traffic-free space spanning two city blocks of shops and eateries – and it is nearly always teeming with people.

The city centre's main shops, from department stores to boutique fashion and accessories outlets, are accessible from the mall and the several shopping arcades that run off it. Also in the mall and its surrounding streets are the city centre's movie theatres and some of Brisbane's best restaurants. The information centre, located mid-mall, can provide you with a guide of things to do around the city.

North-west from the mall are **King George Square** and **Brisbane City Hall**. A short walk through King George Square will take you either left to Roma Street, where the main travel centre for Brisbane is situated, or right and along Wickham Terrace to the **Roma Street Parkland**.

Above, clockwise from left: **Queen Street Mall; Queens Plaza; Queen Street** The mall is a focus of city life, a place to shop, stroll, be entertained or just "people-watch" passing crowds.

Roma Street Parkland overlooks the sprawling inner suburbs of Spring Hill and Petrie Terrace. These were the city's first suburban residential areas and a walking tour reveals many streets containing elegant houses built in the 19th century.

To the north-east, you can pay your respects to Brisbane's war heroes at **Anzac Square**, with its symbolic **Eternal Flame of Remembrance**.

South of the mall, stroll across the river on the Goodwill Bridge, near the **City Botanic Gardens**, to enjoy excellent views from the Kangaroo Point Cliffs; then take a stroll back along the river up to **South Bank**.

Clockwise from top left: **Post Office Square; Riverside Walkway at Kangaroo Point; Walking and bicycling on the Goodwill Bridge** Kangaroo Point's Riverside Walkway along the top of the Kangaroo Point cliffs provides a great view of the river and city centre.

Eastward from the mall is the commercial and business precinct of the city, a place of towering office buildings along lower Queen Street, Creek and Eagle Streets. Every Sunday from 8 a.m. to 4 p.m. shoppers search for uniquely crafted bargains at the **Eagle Street Pier Art and Craft Market**.

At the top of the mall, beside the river, is the **Treasury Casino**. The casino, in the former government treasury offices, is open 24-hours a day for entertainment, dining and gaming.

The great loop of the Brisbane River that embraces three sides of the city centre allows for sightseeing from the bridges that span the river, or from pleasure craft on the water. The on-water choice is between the passenger ferries and a number of tour cruises that operate from North Quay and **Eagle Street Pier**. Swift **CityCat** ferries operate a service along the river from the University of Queensland to Newstead – a mesmerising journey at night when the river sparkles with reflections of the city's lights.

Things to See and Do

1 Catch a film at the plush Regent Cinema
2 Laze in the lush City Botanic Gardens
3 Take a tour down the river at night
4 Rock climb at Kangaroo Point Cliffs
5 Visit the Maritime Museum
6 Enjoy street performances at South Bank

Clockwise from top: **Riverside centre from the Story Bridge; Eagle Street Pier; Riverside Markets** Eagle Street mixes business with entertainment and a cluster of riverside restaurants and cafés. It is host to the colourful and popular Eagle Street Pier Art and Craft Market, and paddlewheeler river cruises depart from Eagle Street Pier.

Another way to enjoy the river is by visiting the **Riverlife Adventure Centre** (Ph: 07 3891 5766) just across from the City Botanic Gardens. The centre is based below the Kangaroo Point Cliffs at the Old Naval Stores, and its activities include kayaking, mountain-bike riding, rock climbing and abseiling.

Along the top of the cliffs at Kangaroo Point is a walk with spectacular views over the city. It is a great place to watch the sun set behind the city buildings and the mountains of Brisbane Forest Park to the west.

As in most Australian cities, sport is a passion in Brisbane. Close to the city centre are the famous "Gabba", where cricket and Australian football are played, and Rugby League's Queensland home, **Suncorp Stadium**. Within easy travelling distance are Rugby Union's **Ballymore** and two racecourses where punters can try their luck – **Eagle Farm** and **Doomben**.

Right, top to bottom: **Suncorp Stadium; Water sports on the River** Recreational activities abound and sports of all kinds are practised in Brisbane.

City Botanic Gardens

Take George, Albert or Edward Streets southward from the Queen Street Mall and you come to the City Botanic Gardens, a place of sprawling lawns and shady trees from around Australia and the world. Many of the trees still growing today were planted when Brisbane was established, making the gardens the cradle of horticulture in Queensland and a truly historic part of the city.

The gardens were created in 1855 on the site of the "Government Garden", where food crops were grown for the Moreton Bay penal settlement. The gardens' first superintendent, Walter Hill, set up an experimental farm where settlers could learn gardening and crop management so the colony could become self-sufficient. One of Hill's major roles was to plant and assess the suitability of native and exotic plants for South-East Queensland's climate and soils, including sugar cane, tobacco and pineapples. He also planted ornamental shrubs and trees that thrive today as mature plants up to 150 years old. These include bunya and hoop pines, macadamia from the region's forests, Moreton Bay figs (the fig native to South-East Queensland) and the first jacaranda tree (brought from South America).

Lawns, trees and ornamental ponds with the modern city as a backdrop In many parts of the City Botanic Gardens tall trees and colourful flower gardens shield the visitor from any hint of a bustling city close by.

Ponds, fringed by palms and flowering shrubs, attract many species of birds The ponds in this central part of the gardens are part of a creek that once ran down from the city centre.

Over the years, the gardens have been home to a zoo, an aviary, tennis courts, extensive ponds and a tea house but, with the exception of some of the ponds, these are now long gone. The existing ponds include one with a sculpture of a man with two brolgas in its centre. The pond was built in the 1950s by gardens director Harry Oakman as a "billabong" and like the gardens' other ponds it attracts resident lungfish, catfish, eels, herons, pied cormorants, black ducks, wood ducks, ibis, moorhens and kingfishers.

Recreation and picnics on the lawns underneath majestic trees More information on the gardens' many plant species can be obtained from the rotunda inside the Albert Street gates.

Stroll along the river walk, shaded by native fig trees The perfect place to relax and gaze at the lazy river traffic and bobbing sailing boats moored off Gardens Point.

Mangroves in the City

Thanks to a mud bank left by the disastrous 1974 Brisbane flood, the City Botanic Gardens have a naturally growing mangrove foreshore on the very tip of Gardens Point – allowing nature to flourish in the heart of the city.

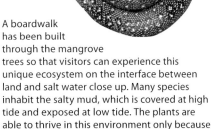

A boardwalk has been built through the mangrove trees so that visitors can experience this unique ecosystem on the interface between land and salt water close up. Many species inhabit the salty mud, which is covered at high tide and exposed at low tide. The plants are able to thrive in this environment only because

the underside of their leaves excrete salt, which would otherwise build up and kill them. The intertwined protective roots and branches of these mangroves provide homes and safe breeding sites for both marine and land birds and animals, including ghost crabs (*left*) and diamond pythons (*above right*).

Recreation in the Gardens

The City Botanic Gardens are open 24-hours a day and are a tranquil place to escape the hectic rush of the city. You can stroll the lawns and shady pathways, sit on the riverside benches beneath giant Moreton Bay figs, enjoy watching birds in the trees and the ponds, appreciate sculptures or dine at the **City Gardens Café**, built in 1903 and once the curator's residence. Special places include a bamboo grove, rainforest, mangroves, ornamental gardens and formal gardens.

Volunteers lead free, guided walks at 11 a.m. and 1 p.m. daily, except for Sundays, public holidays and mid-December to mid-January. The one-hour tour gives visitors the opportunity to learn about the plants, wildlife and history of the gardens. Guides meet at the main rotunda opposite the Albert Street gates (Ph: 07 3403 8888 for information). The **River Stage**, built in 1989, replaces the old 1950s bandstand and is used regularly for free entertainment. Other parts of the gardens are also used for community events throughout the year.

Sculpture in the Gardens

The City Botanic Gardens provides a perfect site for public sculpture and has several important pieces on permanent display. One of the sculptures with a historic flavour is the **flood marker**, set in the lowest point in the gardens, behind the rotunda at the Albert Street entrance. It depicts the chaos of flood debris surrounding a vertical post that is marked with the Brisbane River's flood levels of 1890, 1893, 1897 and 1974. Eight major floods have swept though the gardens since 1870.

Another series of bronze sculptures portray life-size and life-like kangaroos, which appear to laze in the shade of trees that fringe the open lawns sloping down to the River Stage.

Left to right: **The gardens are a showcase for sculpture, from historical to contemporary** Jemmy Morrill & the Brolgas (*left*) celebrates the life of Jemmy (James) Morrill, the lone survivor of a shipwreck in north Queensland in 1846 who lived with Aborigines for 17 years; Morning Star (*centre*) at the Parliament House end of the gardens, was created by eminent American sculptor John Barlow-Hudson; The flood marker (*right*) shows the water levels reached during Brisbane's four major floods. In the 1974 flood, water rose up 4.6 m in the centre of the gardens. Whole collections of plants were destroyed and the gardens were closed for ten weeks.

City Hall and King George Square

The heritage-listed Brisbane City Hall, one of the city's finest buildings, was opened in 1930 after a six-year construction. Until the high-rise era, the City Hall was the tallest building in Brisbane and its 92-m Clock Tower dominated the city skyline. Today, with King George Square in front and streets to its left and right, the building still stands out as the centrepoint of the city.

The sandstone-faced structure on a granite base has an imposing front of tall Corinthian columns supporting a massive triangular pediment with a relief sculpture depicting early settlement. Until 1966, the area in front of City Hall was part of Albert Street, with traffic divided by the original King George Square – a small, rectangular sandstone island adorned with a pond and statue of King George V on a horse. Opposite were the Tivoli movie theatre and city office buildings. In 1966, the street was closed, the old square razed, the Tivoli and its neighbouring buildings removed and the new 72 m by 88 m King George Square (with a multi-level carpark underneath) was constructed level with the entrance to City Hall. The George V statue now stands to the right of the City Hall entrance, and in 1988 a bronze sculpture commemorating the early settlers was placed to the left of the entrance.

King George Square today is a delightful area, paved, grassed and free of traffic. You can relax by the fountain, feed the pigeons and appreciate the beauty of the City Hall building in its entirety.

King George Square and City Hall The broad, open King George Square allows the architectural beauty of City Hall to be enjoyed. The square, a popular place for celebrations and rallies, is home to four highly polished bronze sculptures by Italian artist Arnaldo Pomodoro. The works were a feature of Brisbane's World Expo in 1988 and were installed permanently in the square in 1991.

Left to right: **The Petrie Tableau; City Hall by night; Speakers Corner sculpture group** The Petrie Tableau, erected in 1988 for Australia's Bicentenary, depicts the early settler Andrew Petrie setting off on an exploratory journey of the Moreton Bay region in 1842; The beauty of City Hall can truly be appreciated when the building is illuminated at night; The Speakers Corner figures are author Steele Rudd, one-time premier Sir Charles Lilley and women's activist Emma Miller.

View from the Clock Tower

A trip up the restored antique lift to the top of the 92-m City Hall Clock Tower rewards the visitor with an all-round view of Brisbane city. From high above the surrounding streets you are face-to-face with the city's high-rise office blocks. Between them peek the sprawling suburbs and the wide reaches of the river. Bookings are not needed for Clock Tower visits. This view is looking northward towards Roma Street Station and the Roma Street Parkland.

Things to See and Do

1 Brisbane City Hall Clock Tower Tour

2 Visit the Museum of Brisbane (Ph: 07 3403 8888)

3 Check out a concert at the City Hall Auditorium

4 Take a short walk across Wickham Terrace to the Roma Street Parkland

5 Relax by the fountain and ponder its many decorative sculptures

Inside City Hall

The most spectacular feature of the interior of City Hall is its magnificent circular **auditorium** topped by an impressive domed ceiling decorated with ornate relief sculptures. The auditorium has a permanent stage and seats up to 1500 people, making it a popular venue for concerts, conferences, dinners, balls, flower shows and community events. Throughout the year many free concerts and performances are also held in the auditorium as part of the **City Entertainment Program**, and many solo performances utilise the auditorium's **heritage-listed pipe organ**. City Hall also has seven other function rooms that are available for public and private functions.

The entrance to City Hall from King George Square is through a high-ceilinged, marbled foyer with a white marble staircase leading to the first floor and the auditorium's dress circle. Wide, curving hallways circle the auditorium on both levels and lead to offices and other function rooms.

City Hall contains the **Brisbane City Council meeting chambers** and the **offices of the Lord Mayor and councillors**. It once housed most of the council's administration offices, but these are now in the Brisbane Administration Centre behind City Hall.

Tours of Brisbane City Hall (Ph: 07 3403 8888) include a trip up the Clock Tower and are conducted on weekdays from 8.30 a.m. to 4.30 p.m.

Museum of Brisbane

The City Hall is also home to the Museum of Brisbane, which celebrates Brisbane's history, heritage and culture in its constantly updated, informative exhibitions.

Museum of Brisbane Social history, artistic and cultural displays celebrate Brisbane's past, its lifestyle and its people.

Displays in five exhibition spaces combine social history with visual arts, craft and design, featuring the work of local and international artists. If you're an art lover, you can purchase works created by local artists from the museum's gift shop.

The museum is situated on the ground floor of City Hall and is open daily from 10 a.m. to 5 p.m. Entry is free and free guided tours of exhibitions are available on Tuesday, Thursday and Saturday at 11 a.m.

Main Auditorium, City Hall The elaborately decorated Main Auditorium is able to seat up to 1500 people in opulent comfort.

From top: **Sculpture in King George Square** *Ambition, Power,* and *Machine* – three of the four polished bronze works by Italian sculptor Arnaldo Pomodoro.

Gardens to Enjoy

Roma Street Parkland is a garden lover's paradise with distinct regions displaying a wide range of Australian and exotic plants.

Displays range from arid climate succulents to rainforest ferns and coastal wetland species.

A beautiful, ever-changing display of annuals in the aptly named Spectacle Garden is a centrepiece of the parkland.

Winter is a particularly good time to see blooms – camellias and azaleas, native violets, bird of paradise, gymea lilies and Bangkok rose.

In other seasons, plants are chosen to suit the climate, including Brisbane's hot, humid midsummer.

The Spectacle Garden is therefore an excellent guide to what annuals will thrive at different times of the year in Queensland.

Lilies on the lake enhance the atmosphere of tranquillity.

Cyclamen add to the vibrant display of colour in the parkland.

Pansies festoon the sculpture trellis in the Spectacle Garden.

Roma Street Parkland

Roma Street Parkland is claimed to be the world's largest subtropical garden in a city centre and is a fitting complement to Brisbane's two other public landscaped places – the City Botanic Gardens and South Bank Parklands. The Roma Street Parkland begins just a short walk from King George Square, and runs up Wickham Terrace and west almost to Countess Street in Petrie Terrace, with an entrance from **Roma Street Station**.

Roma Street Parkland incorporates the high, sloping lawns and trees of the old Albert Park, defined by a dog-leg in Wickham Terrace where it swings off the ridge of Spring Hill to meet Albert Street. Below this high part of the parkland are newly landscaped areas that were once the Roma Street railway goods yard. The unsightly conglomeration of sheds, rail lines, goods wagons and trucks on flat, dusty land has been transformed into a garden oasis close to the city centre.

A large, curving drive from Roma Street Station to Wickham Terrace surrounds the southern and western side of the parkland, allowing easy access to parking on the parkland's fringes and in a carpark on the western side. Vehicle access at the station end is off Roma Street and walking access is through the station's pedestrian tunnel to platform 10.

Roma Street Parkland is a place for people – lots of people. It has more than a dozen large and small areas for public gatherings, ranging from the **Celebration Lawn**, which can hold 8000 people, to small, secluded nooks such as the **Flying Duck**, for 50 people. The Celebration Lawn is a popular place to hold large public functions, such as the annual **Labor Day picnic**.

The parkland is crisscrossed with walkways and paths that lead to something different at every turn. At the centre are the lake precinct and the **Spectacle Garden** where meandering walks lead past the still waters and through gardens of brilliant annual flowering plants.

Wall of epiphytes A display of various epiphytes, which grow up and around other plants yet are not parasitic, is found in the Spectacle Garden. The wall's openings show vistas of the spring cascade that flows behind.

Past and Present

The Roma Street Parkland is a beautiful blend of the old with the new in what is a historic part of Brisbane. Part of the site was once the centre of Queensland's railway network; the rest – a sloping, sparsely forested area running up to Wickham Terrace, was once Albert Park, one of the city's oldest parks. The Albert Park area has been refurbished, but the 1000-seat amphitheatre and large sculptures that were features of the park for many years remain. The area has been renamed the **Amphitheatre Precinct** and the covered stage with its open seating and spacious grassy lawns continues its role as a place of public entertainment.

Spectacle Garden In the centre of the Roma Street Parkland, the garden is a spectacle of colour, bright with flowering annuals. Continual planting throughout the year means the garden always has a show of flowers that thrive in Brisbane's subtropical climate.

Near the Albert Street entrance to the parkland are **Spring Hill Corner** and **Sunset Glade**, both higher vantage points that give views of the parkland, Roma Street transit centre and the city. From here, pathways lead to the **Amphitheatre** and the central **Spectacle Garden**, from where you can continue your walk around the lake, along a rocky lakeside peninsula, through a forest of paperbarks and a gully lined with ferns, then on to the upper parkland and Wickham Terrace entrance.

Another walk that is well worth the stroll is the **Art Walk**, which tells the story of the area from Aboriginal meeting place to rail yard, cattle market to public park, all through the artwork of 16 talented Queensland artists. For those wanting to step back in time, behind the parkland, on Wickham Terrace at Spring Hill, are many 19th-century houses and the city's oldest building – **The Windmill** on Wickham Terrace, built in 1828. If you are more inclined to laze than walk, among the parkland's facilities are picnic tables, barbecues and children's playgrounds for relaxed family outings.

Left to right: **Stepping stones around the lake; Jelly Bean Train; Fern Gully** The parkland has a variety of themes from stepping stones by the lake to a forest of paperbarks and a damp gully with profusely growing ferns. The Jelly Bean Train rides are a popular way of getting around the 16-ha gardens.

South Brisbane and West End

In the 1820s, despite being cut off from the convict settlement known as Moreton Bay by a wide, flowing stream, the southern bank of the Brisbane River was still seen as a logical site for expansion. Twenty years later, when Brisbane was opened to free settlers, the south bank was declared a "warehousing port". The deepwater frontage of the southside led to it becoming one of the fledgling city's major wharf areas – a rabble of hotels, stores, warehouses, butcher shops, blacksmiths, stables and huts. After the first **Victoria Bridge** was built in the 1850s, the southside grew quickly, soon spreading over a triangle of land formed by a great loop of the river. These areas are today the suburbs of **South Brisbane**, **West End** and **Highgate Hill**, where many of the city's most popular artistic and cultural attractions are situated.

South Bank Parklands Developed on the site of Expo 88, South Bank has become a lively mix of entertainment, restaurants and recreation along the riverside. Expo, the Queensland Cultural Centre and South Bank have been the catalyst for the development and renewal of the city's southside.

In the 1960s, dilapidated foreshore buildings south of the river were removed to create a riverside park, now known as **South Bank Parklands**. Remnants of the old era can be seen in South Bank's restored **Plough Inn Hotel** and the **Allgas Building** (built as Allan and Stark's first drapery store).

In the 1980s, construction of the **Queensland Cultural Centre** and the staging of **World Expo 88** initiated over a decade of development and growth in the area, turning South Brisbane into a lively, modern, residential, recreation and commercial precinct.

South Bank Markets A regular attraction for visitors to South Bank is the Art and Craft Market held on Friday from 5 p.m. to 10 p.m. Saturday 11 a.m. to 5 p.m. and Sunday 9 a.m. to 5 p.m.

City Beach The white sand and azure waters of South Bank's artificial beach create the feeling of a seaside retreat, yet just across the river are the enticements of the busy, bustling city.

Conventions and Exhibitions

A sign of maturity for any city is a major facility in which to stage national and international exhibitions and conventions – and Brisbane has achieved this with the modern **Convention and Exhibition Centre** at South Bank.

The complex covers two blocks of South Brisbane and stages year-round events ranging from pop concerts to motor shows. It is a multifunctional building that can accommodate up to 8000 people for a wide range of events, including banquets for 1380 people and silver-service banquets for up to 300. The **Great Hall** seats up to 4000 and there are 21 all-purpose meeting rooms. The centre also boasts a spacious outdoor terrace with a city skyline view.

South Brisbane Town Hall Built in 1892 when the city was divided into a number of municipalities, this sandstone and brick building is a fine example of Italian classical revival style. It is now part of Somerville House school.

Things to See and Do

1 View the exhibits at the Queensland Art Gallery (Ph: 07 3840 7303)

2 See a show at the Queensland Performing Arts Complex (Ph: 07 3840 7444)

3 Visit the Qld Museum's TryScience Kiosk (Ph: 07 3840 7635)

4 Check out an event at the Brisbane Convention and Exhibition Centre (Ph: 07 3308 3000)

5 Swim or sunbathe at South Bank's artificially created City Beach, or enjoy the nearby South Bank Markets

Queensland Cultural Centre

A pleasant walk from the mall across Victoria Bridge leads to the Queensland Cultural Centre – a group of modern, like-designed buildings that form the hub of Brisbane's art world.

The Performing Arts Complex stages a variety of theatrical and artistic extravaganzas in its three theatres. Queensland Art Gallery exhibits work of art ranging from Picasso to Pacific Island craft. Nearby, the Queensland Museum displays a range of exhibits from dinosaurs to historic aeroplanes.

The Cultural Centre also houses the State Library, Queensland Conservatorium of Music and the Queensland Gallery of Modern Art. Buses from the city and suburbs stop at the Cultural Centre stop, making it easy for visitors to find.

Queensland Museum A Tricerotops model delights visitors to the museum's dinosaur garden, where life-size models of several dinosaurs inhabit a realistic rainforest setting.

Queensland Performing Arts Complex The Cremorne Theatre, Lyric Theatre, Playhouse and QPAC Studios offer year-round shows to amuse and entertain theatre-goers.

Performing Arts Complex South Bank's entertainment venue for musicals, plays, opera, ballet and rock concerts is on par with any in the world.

Brisbane's international standing received two major boosts when the city staged the 1982 Commonwealth Games and World Expo 88.

Riverfront land, mostly housing tumble-down industrial buildings between Vulture and Melbourne Streets, was transformed into the Expo 88 fairground.

The event attracted visitors from all over the world and some of Expo's attractions still grace South Bank.

Nepalese Peace Pagoda
An Expo 88 exhibit, the pagoda marks South Bank's entrance.

South Bank Markets Jewellery, knick-knacks, souvenirs and giftware tempt shoppers.

Dining on the boardwalk
Cafés and restaurants offer river views and a variety of cuisines.

Bougainvillea-covered Arbour This pretty, flower-filled walkway snakes through the heart of South Bank.

South Bank Parklands and South Brisbane Walks

While the river bank on the city side is cluttered by the busy Riverside Expressway, the southern bank is a tranquil place designed to allow people to appreciate the city's cultural charms. Here, South Bank Parklands and the **Queensland Cultural Centre** give you a place in which to relax and enjoy entertainment varying from street performance to opera.

South Bank Parklands are the place to stroll along boardwalks and pathways, including the shade-dappled arbour which runs the length of the complex and is resplendent with bougainvillea blossoms. An afternoon can be whiled away reclining by the **beach** or on the lawns, eating and drinking at the many restaurants, cafés and bars, fossicking through the colourful **markets**, or watching buskers perform in the **Piazza**.

As well as the **Arbour Walk**, take the riverside boardwalk that runs the full length of the parklands and extends past the Queensland Cultural Centre to the parks and walkways of the West End river bank. Behind the main section of South Bank Parklands lies Grey Street, filled with eateries, a cinema complex, the **Queensland College of Art** and the **Queensland Conservatorium of Music**. Farther back, international hotels, apartment buildings, office complexes and the **Brisbane Convention and Exhibition Centre** line Merivale Street.

Cordelia Street runs parallel with Merivale and adjoins one of the city's oldest parks – **Musgrave Park**. The park hosts numerous events throughout the year and is a place of special significance for many Indigenous Australians, with facilities dedicated to the promotion and preservation of Aboriginal heritage and culture.

South Bank Lagoon Shallow, crystal-clear waters make the lagoon popular with kids.

City Beach

Easily one of South Bank's most enjoyable places, particularly in the warmer months, is the beach. Although artificial, it is more than just a swimming pool; there are no tiles, just sparkling blue water over clean white sand. You could be fooled into thinking you were at the seaside but for the city's tall buildings visible across the river.

There is no surf and no salty sea breeze but splashing in the cool water or lazing in the sun is as close as you can get to a day at the beach whilst still being in the city.

South Bank Surf Patrol Qualified lifesavers patrol the beach to protect swimmers.

Maritime Museum Past the beach, at the southern end of South Bank Parklands near the Goodwill Bridge, is the Queensland Maritime Museum. Its collection includes several ships, a lighthouse and artefacts and records documenting nearly two centuries of the State's sailing and boating history.

South Brisbane to West End

With a skyline dominated by the spiked tower of the **Expo Needle** and numerous new high-rise apartment blocks, the suburb of West End is just a short walk or bus ride from South Brisbane. The rejuvenation of South Brisbane that began in the 1980s soon spread to the surrounding suburbs of West End and **Highgate Hill** – suburbs that are now chic residential areas complete with fashionable restaurants frequented by young, upwardly mobile Brisbanites. While the booming real estate market has led to many old buildings being replaced by modern structures, those with heritage value are being preserved or restored to their original form. Dwellings range from modest workers' cottages to elegant Queenslander-style houses on high stumps. When you wander through South Brisbane, West End, Highgate Hill and **Dutton Park**, it's easy to imagine how the place might have looked a century or more ago.

Gas Stripping Tower A relic of the days when the people of Brisbane used reticulated coal gas for cooking and hot water, the tower is now preserved as a historic structure in Davies Park at West End.

Expo Needle This colourful tower was a feature of Expo 88, creating a laser light show over the city each night of the event. After Expo, it was bought by hairdressing doyen Stefan and moved to his South Brisbane office.

A walk down **Boundary Street**, West End, is truly a cosmopolitan experience. West End is a multicultural community with Greek, Italian, Indian, Middle Eastern, Chinese and Vietnamese restaurants, and shop after shop of exotic foods, furnishings, clothing and giftware.

Dutton Park, to the south-east, is the site of Brisbane's infamous **Boggo Road Gaol** (150–160 Annerley Road, Dutton Park, Ph: 07 3846 7423 for entry fee), where ghosts of hanged murderers are said to roam. The gaol is now a historical site and museum, its 19th-century buildings preserving artefacts from its past. In the nearby **South Brisbane Cemetery** are the graves of some of the prisoners who met their demise in the gaol.

Wild Residents of Brisbane

All along the banks of the Brisbane River are parks and gardens that shelter a variety of native wildlife, particularly possums, birds and reptiles. But the most conspicuous residents, drawn to the pungent allure of trees in full fruit, are colonies of noisy flying foxes *(right)*.

At dusk thousands of these fruit- and blossom-eating bats leave their colonies to seek food. They can be seen flying over most suburbs, or heard raucously squabbling in the treetops, and are a popular spotlighting target for wildlife enthusiasts.

Major colonies are on Indooroopilly Island, a conservation park on the river near Long Pocket, and in riverside parkland at West End.

Creative West End Street landscaping in Boundary Street led to this unique "creature" sculpture.

Boundary Street, West End This colourful, cosmopolitan street offers something for everyone.

Dutton Park Mansion A fine example of the Queenslander-style homes that are a feature of the Highgate Hill and Dutton Park area.

Fortitude Valley to New Farm

In the 1840s and 50s, as the convict era drew to a close, early Brisbane experienced a rush of free settlers, which caused the city to expand rapidly. With the river constraining the city on two sides, the only room for growth was northward to Spring Hill and north-east to Fortitude Valley and New Farm. In 1849, hundreds of migrants boarded three ships chartered by the Reverend Dr John Dunmore Lang, who had promised free land to start a new life. When they arrived, they found that land was not available and took up residence in camps. Many settlers from the ship *Fortitude* camped in what became known as "Fortitude Valley". By the 1880s, Fortitude Valley was densely settled and, when a rail line from the city was built in 1891, it became a major retail and commercial centre, reaching its zenith in the 1950s and 60s.

The Valley

Fortitude Valley – or "the Valley" as it is known – is today undergoing a style resurgence that may see it regain its glory days. In the 1950s, the big shopping emporium of James McWhirter – on the "Valley Corner" of Wickham and Brunswick Streets – and nearby rival T.C. Beirne's turned the Valley into Brisbane's principal shopping area. When the big department stores left to set up in modern, suburban shopping centres, the Valley went into decline, becoming a place of run-down shops

by day and nightclubs, pubs, massage parlours and tattooist shops by night. In recent decades, formerly dilapidated buildings have been restored for use as shops, galleries and residential units. **Chinatown Mall** and **Brunswick Street Mall** were established and, with inner-city living becoming popular, large blocks of modern apartments sprang up around the Valley and New Farm. The **nightclubs** are still there and beat with the rhythm of hundreds of eager clubbers on weekends. And while some back streets still have unsavoury reputations, the hotels and clubs have largely re-invented themselves to attract a young, hip clientele. Upmarket restaurants, coffee shops, bookshops and galleries are also multiplying.

New Farm

During the convict period, scrub was cleared east of the city on the bank of the Brisbane River so that the rich soil could be used for farming. It was called New Farm to distinguish it from older areas. When free settlers flocked to Brisbane, the demand for fresh produce increased and New Farm became important for fruit, vegetables, grains and dairy products. Suburbia eventually squeezed out the farmers and the influx of European immigrants after World War II turned New Farm into a culturally diverse community.

Once a precinct of woolstores, warehouses and wharves, New Farm and neighbouring **Newstead** are now becoming prime residential areas.

The Valley Corner, where Wickham Street and Brunswick Street cross is towered over by the tall, red-brick building of the old McWhirter's emporium – from days when the Valley was one of Brisbane's prestige shopping places.

Brunswick St Mall Starting outside the historic McWhirter's building at the Valley Corner is the paved block of Brunswick Street Mall. Market stalls at the mall's weekend markets sell everything from fresh produce to jewellery and clothing.

Chinatown Celebrating Chinese culture in Brisbane, Chinatown is a colourful place to visit. A block in central Fortitude Valley, running parallel to Brunswick Street Mall, has been turned into Chinatown Mall, with Asian restaurants and shops selling oriental wares.

New Farm Park

In spring, when roses and jacarandas are in bloom, one of the city's prettiest and most popular parks becomes carpeted in purple petals. New Farm Park's great circular drive is lined with jacarandas that are almost 100 years old. Then there's the roses – 14,000 of them in 300 varieties, planted in ordered beds. Add to this the rich, red exuberance of large poincianas in flower and many-hued bougainvilleas, and New Farm Park, once the site of a racecourse, is truly a floral fantasy.

The park is not just a nice spot for "Green Thumbs", you can take advantage of the grassy **picnic and barbecue areas** and kids love climbing along the rope ladders that link a row of giant Moreton Bay fig trees.

New Farm Park jacarandas These exotic trees, originally from South America, have become a feature of Brisbane. Each spring, New Farm Park is one of the best places to experience their beauty.

Things to See and Do

1 Enjoy yum-cha in one of the Valley's Chinese restaurants

2 Attend the September Moon Festival in Chinatown Mall, when lion dances and fireworks bring the valley to life

3 Take an Art Circuit walk through the more than 15 art galleries and exhibition spaces in New Farm or visit the Brisbane Powerhouse, which offers a variety of shows and exhibitions (Ph: 07 3358 8622)

4 Catch a live gig at The Zoo or dance to DJs in one of the many clubs

Above: **View over the Brisbane River to New Farm Park with the city centre in the background.**
1. Brisbane City **2.** New Farm Park **3.** Powerhouse Centre for the Arts **4.** Fortitude Valley

The Powerhouse

A disused coal-burning powerhouse that once generated electricity for Brisbane's trams and homes is now one of the city's premier venues for the **live arts**.

The Powerhouse, with parts of the old building retained – including graffiti – and new structures added, is a mid-sized venue for performances, contemporary art and craft exhibitions, conferences and celebrations.

The recycled building incorporates modern performance spaces, rehearsal rooms, indoor and outdoor entertainment and relaxation areas in a delightful location beside New Farm Park on the banks of the Brisbane River.

Right: **New Farm Park's roses and jacarandas** Springtime turns the park into a blaze of colour around the bandstand.

Short Trip – Mt Coot-tha

John Oxley, who explored the Brisbane River in 1823, described Mt Coot-tha as "forest land rising back two miles to a lofty ridge". When the first Europeans climbed this ridge in 1828, one wrote: "The view from south-east to north-west was extensive and very grand, presenting an immense, thinly wooded plain, whose surface was gently undulated, and clothed in luxuriant grass". Today, that plain is the city of Brisbane, and Mt Coot-tha, named after an Aboriginal word *Kuta*, meaning "place of wild honey", is the place visitors flock to for a view of the city.

The Lookout

An easy drive from the city takes you to the top of Mt Coot-tha's southern end where a lookout gives views of the clustered high-rise buildings of the city centre and the **Gateway Bridge** beyond. Reaches of the Brisbane River, as it snakes its way through the city, are visible in the foreground. Beyond the river mouth is **Moreton Bay** and on the eastern horizon is **Moreton Island** with its distinctive white sand blows. To the south, beyond the sprawling suburbs, stand **Mount Tamborine**, the **Lamington Plateau** and the **Border Ranges**. Further to the south-west are **Flinders Peak** near Ipswich and the mountains of the **Scenic Rim** and **Cunninghams Gap** in the **Great Dividing Range**.

Mt Coot-tha Lookout On a clear day you can see a long way from the lookout at the southern end of Mt Coot-tha. The lookout has a cafe, restaurant and souvenir shop set amid the landscaped vantage point.

At the lookout are the **Kuta Café** and the **Summit Restaurant** in the restored Mt Coot-tha tearooms. The site of the lookout, 244 m above sea level, was once called "One Tree Hill" because a lone gum tree was the only tree left standing after timber was cut to make railway sleepers in the 1870s. In 1874, about 607 ha (1500 acres) of the mountain were proclaimed a public park – in stark contrast to its use during World War II, when the US army used parts of the mountain as an ammunitions dump. In 1918, a kiosk was built where the lone tree stood and the mountain became a must-visit place.

In 1960, Brisbane City Council gave permission for the construction of television towers and today Mt Coot-tha is home to four television stations. A sealed road was built along the mountain's crest and down its north-eastern side; this is now a popular tourist drive with many parks and lookouts.

Telescope at the Lookout Visitors to the Mt Coot-tha lookout have an expansive semi-circular paved platform to catch the views to the south, east and north-east. The landscaped area is topped with a central, higher lookout with a plaque showing lines pointing to distant landmarks.

Summit Restaurant and Bar at the Lookout A restored and expanded kiosk and tearooms, built in 1918, give visitors the opportunity to combine fine dining with fine views. At night the lights of the city spread out in a colourful carpet more than 200 m below the restaurant windows and decks.

Aboriginal Art Trail

The Mt Coot-tha Aboriginal Art Trail showcases Aboriginal art in its natural setting. Visitors can learn how Aboriginal art is used as a way of mapping the land and passing on important cultural information.

The trail features eight works of art. This includes the main gallery at the end of the track, which is an Aboriginal map of the whole site. Interpretive signs are provided for you at each location.

The art trail is a 1.8-km loop off the walking trail between the J.C. Slaughter Falls picnic area and the Mt Coot-tha Lookout.

The Brisbane and Ipswich areas were occupied by the Jagera and Turrbal groups. The exact boundaries are not known, but the Turrbal generally occupied the area north of the Brisbane River. Both groups had closely related languages that are classified as belonging to the larger Yaggera language group. Everyday life for the people consisted of hunting and gathering food, with time for games and other social and spiritual activities.

The area, now Brisbane, was known as *Mian-jin*, which means "place shaped like a spike". The Turrbal and the Jagera had numerous campsites, including at the present day suburbs of Woolloongabba, Toowong, Bowen Hills, Newstead, Nundah and Nudgee.

Walking Trails

The forested top of Mt Coot-tha, and the ridges and valleys on its north-eastern side, are crisscrossed with walking trails and dotted with picnic areas. One of the major walking trails begins from **Simpsons Falls Park** picnic area in a valley on the north-east side of the mountain. The trail, up West Ithaca Creek to the top of Mt Coot-tha near the **Channel 7** and **Channel 9** studios, is through typical eucalypt scrub. Another major trail begins at the **J.C. Slaughter Falls Park** on the eastern side and takes you up the central, 258-m **Constitution Hill**.

Just on the southern side of the Channel 9 studios (the first television station on the road from the lookout), is a picnic area with a short walking track down to an old gold mine. Prospectors first started looking for gold on Mt Coot-tha in the late 1800s and reports detail mines being worked there in 1893, 1933 and 1939. Mining gave the area one of its enduring place names – Gold Creek – but was stopped in the 1950s and reports indicate that not much gold was found!

Above left: **Mountains in the distance** A lookout to the south-west from a Mt Coot-tha walking trail looks towards Ipswich, the Great Dividing Range and Cunninghams Gap. *Above right:* **The top of Mt Coot-tha has many walking trails**, with places of interest including an old gold mine and Aboriginal heritage displays. Mt Coot-tha is a Brisbane City Council reserve that is part of the Brisbane Forest Park complex of reserves, State forests and national parks, which stretches more than 100 km to the north-west along the D'Aguilar Range.

Lakeside picnics The gardens have extensive manicured lawn areas for picnics or relaxing.

Shady lawns beside the water One of the many water features of the gardens.

Lilies and ducks on the lake Ponds throughout the gardens attract many kinds of wildlife.

Lakeside walks Paths wind past palm-fringed ponds.

Short Trip – Brisbane Botanic Gardens

In the wooded foothills of Mt Coot-tha, on the city's western fringe, is a spectacular botanic garden that is one of Australia's premier public gardens. Here, amongst the original tall eucalypts of the 52 ha site, visitors can see examples of native Australian bushland, rainforest and grassland as well as viewing plant varieties from around the world.

Brisbane City seen from the Gardens Lookout A pleasant high point in the Brisbane Botanic Gardens at Mt Coot-tha offers a great view of Brisbane, particularly of skyscrapers in the city centre. It is the perfect half-way point on your tour of the gardens.

The Brisbane Botanic Gardens at Mt Coot-tha, just 7 km from the city centre, showcase 25 ha of exotic plants and 27 ha of Australian plants in themed displays along a maze of pathways. Special areas include an **Australian and exotic rainforest**, an **arid zone** and **cactus house**, a **temperate garden**, a **bamboo grove** and a **fragrant plant and herb garden**. As well as the Australian rainforest, plant communities represented include temperate wetlands, heathland, open eucalypt woodlands and savanna grasslands. Many of the native plants in the gardens are rare or endangered in their natural habitat and a conservation section has more than 40 rare or threatened species.

A special **Aboriginal Plant Trail** explores the Australian rainforest area and gives you an insight into the relationship that exists between Aborigines and the forest, while the exotic rainforest has trees, shrubs and vines from some of the world's great jungles.

Tropical Wonders

One of the gardens' landmarks is the giant **Tropical Dome**, where the atmosphere is kept warm and moist in order to grow amazing plants from the jungles of the world. A pathway winds up through the geodesic dome around a central pond that contains the world's largest water lilies, from the Amazon, with pads 1 m wide and a 20 cm bloom. The path is lined with shrubs, epiphytes, herbs and trees. A large lake nearby, surrounded by trees and lawns, has scores of wild ducks and other water birds as well as turtles and lizards.

Totems at the lakeside These 1.5 m to 6 m tall totems signify Aboriginal, Druidic, American Indian, Norse and Melanesian cultures.

Ferns and Cactuses

Over 80 different varieties of ferns are kept in the moist fern house. To the other extreme is the arid zone garden, which displays the cactuses and plants of the dry and desert regions of the world.

Tropical Dome Creating a tropical rainforest atmosphere inside and an arid zone outside.

Sir Thomas Brisbane Planetarium

The city's first planetarium, built at the gardens in 1978, is a window to the universe. You experience the cosmos in virtual form in spectacular film shows of Brisbane's night sky projected onto the inside of the planetarium's Cosmic Skydome; or you can see the stars and planets in reality through telescopes in the planetarium's observatory.

The Planetarium, like the city, is named after Sir Thomas Brisbane, Governor of New South Wales in the 1820s. He established Australia's first significant observatory in Sydney and was responsible for the first extensive mapping of the southern sky. His observations led to a list of 7385 stars.

An original copy of his "Brisbane Catalogue of Stars" and one of his telescopes is on display at the planetarium.

The planetarium runs sessions for the public and also has special programs for school groups. Bookings are required for shows in the Cosmic Skydome or to visit the observatory (Ph: 07 3403 8888).

A Taste of Japan

One of the highlights of the Botanic Gardens is the **Japanese Garden**. A tea house beside a pond surrounded by a traditional garden with the key elements of stone, water, meandering paths and vegetation blend harmoniously to create a place of beauty and tranquillity. The theme of the garden is *tsuki-yama-chisen* or mountain-pond-stream. Its path follows an S-shaped curve, so as you approach one vegetation area the view of the next section is hidden – adding mystery and surprise to the garden's many delights. The best time to enjoy its serenity is early morning, when the gardens are less busy.

Adjacent is a **Bonsai House** with almost 100 examples of the ancient Japanese art of creating miniature trees, some of which are more than 80 years old. The Bonsai House is made from rammed earth walls, using soil from the original site to ensure that it blends into the gardens' environment. The gardens are also home to the **Queensland Herbarium**, which has a catalogued collection of about 660,000 preserved plant specimens, including all known plant species that grow in Queensland. The herbarium is a centre of botanical information and research into the State's native plants.

The Brisbane Botanic Gardens are open every day from 8 a.m. and have an auditorium, a restaurant and a gift shop as well as many picnic and rest areas. They close at 5.30 p.m. from September to March and 5 p.m. from April to August. Entry is free (Ph: 07 3403 8888).

Wildlife at Mt Coot-tha Botanic Gardens

The gardens are alive with native wildlife attracted by the lakes and the foliage of various plants that thrive there.

Waterbirds live in large numbers in and around the ponds that dot the gardens. Fish, eels and several species of turtles thrive in the water, including the Eastern Snake-necked Turtle (*right*).

The most common waterbirds are native ducks, including the Pacific Black Duck (*top left*), mallards, Wood Ducks, divers and even the occasional pelican.

Birdlife also includes flycatchers, such as the Willie Wagtail (*top right*), native pigeons, magpies, currawongs, crows, parrots, Sulphur-crested Cockatoos and miners. Owls are seen occasionally, as are circling Wedge-tailed Eagles.

The undergrowth and thick foliage provides protection for snakes and lizards, including the Eastern Water Dragon and Bearded Dragon (*bottom right*), and the trees are home to possums and sometimes Koalas.

Short Trip – Brisbane Suburbs

As Brisbane threw off the baggage of its infamous birth as a harsh convict settlement, settlers, traders and entrepreneurs flocked to the outpost and the city grew quickly. The compact townships of Brisbane Town – today the central business district – South Brisbane and Kangaroo Point expanded and the emerging city began to take shape. The convict settlement had already paved the way for the start of suburbia by seeking out places with water and good soil for farming. As more and more people arrived, the settlement spread north to **Spring Hill**, east to **Fortitude Valley** and **New Farm**, across **Breakfast Creek**, down river to **Hamilton** and westward along the northern bank of the river to **Paddington**, **Milton** and **Toowong**.

Spring Hill

The timber-covered hill to the west of the city, containing a number of good springs, had been used by the convict settlement from 1828 when a windmill was built to grind grain. But by 1856 land was sold along the ridges of Wickham Terrace, and Spring Hill spread to Boundary Street and Gregory Terrace as it became a dormitory suburb for the young city – a role it still plays today, as well as being an important inner-city business and commercial precinct.

Looking over Spring Hill to the city The roofs of cottages from a bygone era contrast with the modern buildings of the city centre. The tip of City Hall's Clock Tower can be seen at top left.

Top to bottom: **Paddington and Bardon suburbs; Iconic Queenslander, Red Hill** One of Brisbane's earliest water towers stands out on the Paddington skyline. These inner suburbs have fine examples of the classic "Queenslander". Paddington also has the Governor's residence, a grand two-storey building from 1865.

Paddington

As demand for housing grew in the late 19th century, the city expanded westward along the ridges of Paddington and **Red Hill**. These inner suburbs have retained much of the character of early Brisbane, as old shops and houses are restored and hold their place against the tide of urban renewal.

Milton

The inner-city riverside suburb of Milton is Rugby League heartland, home to **Suncorp Stadium**, fondly remembered as Lang Park. It also has the landmark **Castlemaine Perkins Fourex brewery** with its neon "XXXX" sign glaring out from the inner-city skyline. Milton's closeness to the city has made it an office suburb with commercial buildings crowding out some old houses. **Park Road** at Milton is also known as a great strip for fine dining.

Outdoor dining at Park Road Renewal and restoration has given inner Brisbane suburbs such as Milton many new entertainment and dining businesses as people enjoy a "village" lifestyle.

Toowong

Set between the slopes of Mount Coot-tha and the Brisbane River, Toowong, once described as "a dense and interminable wilderness of trees and inferior vegetation", became one of Brisbane's early farming areas. When the rail line to Ipswich was built in 1875, Toowong began to develop as a town. Today it is one of the city's finest inner-western suburbs. It has one of Brisbane's grandest homes, **Moorlands**, now part of the Wesley Hospital, as well as the historic **Toowong Cemetery**. The nearby riverside **Regatta Hotel** was where Queensland women first gained entrance to a public bar, although not without outrage when they refused to leave, chaining themselves to the bar.

The Regatta Hotel at Toowong overlooks the river One of the many grand hotels built in the 19th century. The restored three-storey building is noted for its cast-iron lace.

Heritage Hotels

Hotels, many of them grand, ornate buildings, were perhaps the largest single group of buildings to be built in Brisbane's colonial era.

Between 1862 and 1900 more than 100 major hotels were constructed. Many of these well-used watering holes are now gone, such as the magnificent Belle Vue, which stood opposite Parliament House in George Street. But others, including the Regatta Hotel at Toowong and the Breakfast Creek Hotel, remain and have been restored to some of their former glory.

Urban Parrots and Possums

Left: Common Ringtail Possum. *Below right:* Rainbow Lorikeets

Modern Brisbane is a green city and home to a variety of wildlife that exists in harmony with human inhabitants. Many species under threat in other parts of Queensland and Australia live and thrive in the city and surrounds. The Brisbane region has some of the nation's most significant Koala populations in its remaining eucalypt forests, platypuses live in the upper parts of freshwater streams and possums are prolific.

In the past half-century, although the city's growth has destroyed significant amounts of natural habitat, the new suburbs have quickly become "green" as residents established gardens, many with an emphasis on native species. Yards in many older inner-suburbs were often little more than lawn with one shady mango tree, but many have been transformed into wildlife-friendly places. Civic authorities have contributed to parks, gardens and wildlife refuges.

Wherever habitat has been protected or restored the native animals and birds return and thrive. Today, possums, frogs, snakes, lizards, and birds of many kinds can be found in most parts of the city. In more isolated pockets of scrub are Koalas, wallabies, kangaroos, bandicoots and native mice.

Breakfast Creek

This major creek running into the Brisbane River was thus named because the explorer John Oxley stopped for breakfast there on his 1823 journey upriver. Its attractions include the heritage-listed **Breakfast Creek Hotel**, the **Albion Park Paceway** – once the famous thoroughbred racetrack called "The Creek", but now used for trotting and greyhound racing – and the **Temple of the Holy Triad**, built in 1884 by the Cantonese community.

Below, left to right: **Breakfast Creek Hotel; Newstead House** These two fine examples of colonial architecture have been preserved. The 1889 Breakfast Creek Hotel is one of the best. Newstead House, built by grazing pioneer Patrick Leslie, is a National Trust building open to the public.

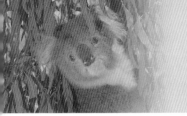

Brisbane Surrounds

Australian
King Parrot

Beyond Brisbane city lie the wide open spaces and blue waters that give life to the region. Places of rich subtropical diversity that once sustained Aborigines are now a mixture of developing cities, growing country towns, farmlands that nourish both livestock and fresh produce, forests and national parks. Five populous cities are located within 100 km of Brisbane's city centre – Redcliffe and Caloundra to the north, Ipswich to the west and Logan and the Gold Coast to the south. Nestled among them are the smaller towns and shires that make up the South-East Queensland jigsaw. East of Brisbane, the blue expanse of Moreton Bay and its sand islands provide idyllic weekend escapes for humans and a haven for wildlife.

History and Heritage

Aborigines occupied the region for more than 10,000 years and some of their heritage endures and is shared in the passing down of cultural lore, such as how the **Glass House Mountains** were formed, and in annual feasts and ceremonies at the **Bunya Mountains**. British explorer James Cook sailed by in 1770, but it was not until 1823 that Moreton Bay and the Brisbane and Pine Rivers were explored by John Oxley. The European era began in 1824 with a convict settlement at **Redcliffe**, which was soon relocated to the northern bank of the Brisbane River on the site of today's central business district. After the penal colony was opened up in 1842, free settlers made their way into districts to the north, west and south, clearing and farming the land and establishing the towns and cities of today.

Forests

Brisbane, a city of parks and gardens, is surrounded by large tracts of natural forest and bushland, preserved for the benefit of residents of the region – the people and the wildlife. Spectacular temperate rainforests cover many of the mountain ranges to the south, west and north, and swathes of eucalypt forests spread over much of the land that has not been farmed. Wallum country of paperbark and banksia scrub, heath-covered swampland running to casuarina-lined beach dunes, or mangrove-covered tidal mudflats cover the coastal land to the east.

Lakes and Rivers

From the ranges west of Brisbane flow the coastal creeks and rivers on which many towns and cities of the region are sited.

The **Brisbane River**, the largest, follows a wide, winding path to Moreton Bay from its source 130 km to the city's north-west in the Brisbane Range near the town of Nanango.

The **Stanley River** begins near the Glass House Mountains and runs south, meeting the Brisbane River near Esk, where two of the region's biggest dams – **Lake Somerset** on the Stanley and Lake Wivenhoe** on the Brisbane – are located. The **Bremer River, South and North Pine Rivers**, Caboolture River and Logan River also grace the region.

Lake Wivenhoe This lake was formed by the construction, in 1985, of Wivenhoe Dam on the Brisbane River near Esk, and is popular for camping, sailing and rowing. It can hold twice as much water as Sydney Harbour!

Top to bottom: **Gooloowan House, Ipswich; Lake Samsonvale from Clear Mountain; Vegetable pickers, Lockyer Valley; Gatton Agricultural College.**

Bays and Islands

Moreton Bay is Brisbane's favourite aquatic playground, a wide expanse of water enclosed by **Bribie and Moreton Islands** to the north, and **North and South Stradbroke Islands** to the south. Beyond swells the South Pacific Ocean. The Bay is a place of many moods – sometimes grey and dark with storms and squalls, sometimes blue and sunny, almost always with a cool sea breeze. It is protected as **Moreton Bay Marine Park**, which extends from Caloundra south to the southernmost tip of South Stradbroke Island and to three nautical miles east of the islands. It is a sanctuary for Dugong, turtles, dolphins and Humpback Whales that pass by on their annual migration to Great Barrier Reef waters and back.

Moreton Bay's waters open into the South Pacific Ocean in three places between the large sand islands. North and South Stradbroke were one island until the 1890s when storm tides scoured the passage at **Jumpinpin**.

The Bay's city foreshore, indented with smaller bays, runs north from the Brisbane River mouth past Brisbane Airport, Nudgee Beach, Shorncliffe and Sandgate to Redcliffe and south past the city's major port complex at **Fisherman**

Top to bottom: **Wellington Point; Cleveland Hotel** The Brisbane region has more than 50 km of foreshore on Moreton Bay, including Redcliffe and Sandgate north of the Brisbane River mouth and Wynnum, Cleveland and Wellington Point to its south. Many of the Bay's beaches and inlets are fringed with mangroves, making them less than ideal for swimming or sunbathing, but excellent for fishing, windsurfing or sailing.

Islands to Wynnum, Manly, Cleveland, Wellington Point, Victoria Point and **Redland Bay**. All along this 50-km stretch you'll find rocky headlands, wide sandy beaches, mangroves and mudflats. Vistas from the many picnic spots and waterfront parks take in the picturesque beauty of the Bay and islands, and there are boat ramps and marinas for mooring and launching all kinds of watercraft.

The northern part of Moreton Bay is mostly open water, much of it shallow with its infamous "chop" proving a hazard for sailors in severe weather. To the south, the Bay is dotted with islands, some inhabited, some not, but most covered with banksia, paperbark or eucalypt scrub and fringed with mangroves or golden sand.

In the central part, off the mouth of the Brisbane River, lie **St Helena Island, Mud Island** and **Green Island**. St Helena Island is national park and contains ruins of a jail from the convict era. Mud Island is a flat, featureless tract barely visible at high tide, and tiny Green Island lives up to its name, being resplendent with lush foliage. **Peel Island** is one of the larger of the Moreton Bay islands. South of it lie the developed islands of **Coochiemudlo, Macleay, Lamb, Karragarra** and **Russell**.

Left to right: **Coochiemudlo Island; Moreton Island; North Stradbroke Island** The islands of Moreton Bay include the large sand islands of Moreton and North and South Stradbroke, populated islands in the central and southern parts and clusters of mangrove-covered islands in the south. Coochiemudlo, just off Victoria Point, has casuarina-fringed bays that attract boating daytrippers. Moreton Island's north-east is dominated by Cape Moreton and its lighthouse, while at Tangalooma, on its central western side, pods of wild Bottlenose Dolphins are frequent visitors. North Stradbroke Island's ocean beaches are popular for camping, fishing, surfing and surfboarding.

Camp Mountain Lookout
With views of the Samford Valley and Glass House Mountains, this is a great place to see how today's terrain is the result of the incredible forces of nature unleashed in the volcanic era.

Driving through the park
Tall eucalypts line the winding road along the D'Aguilar Range.

Jollys Lookout A vantage point in Brisbane Forest Park with views to Moreton Island.

Brisbane Forest Park

The rugged and forested **D'Aguilar Range** is an accessible green region that starts right at the city's back door. This great swathe of dark green ridges and radiating valleys begins at **Mount Coot-tha** – with its landmark television towers 7 km west of the city centre – and stretches north-west for more than 70 km. The area is covered mostly by eucalypt forest as well as significant areas of subtropical rainforest that make it one of South-East Queensland's major natural places. Much of the southern D'Aguilar Range forms Brisbane Forest Park, a 28,500 ha string of national parks, State forests and council reserves linked in a single protected park.

This mountainous country, like most of the present-day terrain of South-East Queensland, owes its origins to the active volcanoes whose mighty lava flows once spewed over the land. During the millions of years since, the softer volcanic rock eroded and left spectacular features, such as the Glass House Mountains, and range upon forested range.

Brisbane Forest Park has many quiet nooks where you can immerse yourself in the natural beauty of the mountains, rivers, creeks and forests, or observe the fascinating wildlife species to which these forests are home.

Maiala Rainforest Teahouse at Mt Glorious
A kookaburra joins patrons on the deck.

Driving the D'Aguilar Range

A visit to Brisbane Forest Park should begin with a call at the park's headquarters nestled near the **Enoggera Reservoir** on the western edge of **The Gap**.

From the park headquarters your drive takes you through tall stands of forest on a narrow, winding, two-lane bitumen road to the mountain townships of **Mount Nebo** and **Mount Glorious**, and

The Crimson Rosella, with its brilliant scarlet and dark blue plumage, is commonly seen in lush forest along the east coast ranges.

beyond. Many picnic places and lookouts with lovely views make the spine of the D'Aguilar Range a pleasant place to while away a lazy afternoon. For bushwalkers and nature-lovers there are well-marked forest trails. From Mount Glorious, you can return to Brisbane eastward via **Samford** or go on to **Wivenhoe Lookout** and west down into the **Brisbane Valley**.

Whipbirds and Bell Miners

The Bell Miner (*left*) is a relative of the common Noisy Miner, but its tinkling call readily distinguishes it from its more rowdy cousins.

Throughout Brisbane Forest Park and the Brisbane Valley, Bell Miners chorus high in the canopy while the shrill whistle-crack of the Eastern Whipbird resounds from the undergrowth. Perhaps the best place to hear these birds is on a short walk from Brisbane Forest Park's headquarters at The Gap along the Araucaria Track beside a bywater of the Enoggera Reservoir.

LEGEND

Major road
Main road
Minor road
Railway
D'Aguilar Range
Scenic Drive
National park

Kilometres
0 10 20 30 km

N

BRIBIE ISLAND NP

MORETON ISLAND NP

North Point
Cape Moreton
Cape Moreton Lighthouse
Comboyuro Point
Bulwer
Mt Tempest
Cowan Cowan
The Desert
Moreton Island
Tangalooma

BLUE LAKE NP
Blue Lake
North Stradbroke Island
Cylinder Beach
Frenchmans Beach
Point Lookout
Flinders Beach
Brown Lake
Dunwich
Amity Point
Amity
Kooringal
Campbell Point
Reeders Point

Russell Island
Peel Island
Coochiemudlo
Macleay Island
Victoria Point
Mount Cotton
Redland Bay
Thornlands
Cleveland Pt
Grandview Hotel
Cleveland
Alexandra Hills
Capalaba
Birkdale

St Helena Island
ST HELENA ISLAND NP
Green Island
Mud Island
Wellington Pt
Wellington Point
Manly
Wynnum

Moreton Bay

Moreton Bay Marine Park

Banksia Beach
Woorim
Bongaree
Bellara
Sandstone Point
Bribie Island
Pumicestone Channel

Goodwin Beach
Ningi
Toorbul
Beachmere
Deception Bay
Scarborough
Redcliffe Pier
Settlement Cove
REDCLIFFE
Clontarf
Bramble Bay
Brighton
Sandgate
Shorncliffe
Boondall Wetlands

FRESHWATER NP

Donnybrook
Elimbah
Wamuran
Caboolture Aerodrome
Burpengary
Narangba
Lake Kurwongbah
Dakabin
Kallangur
Petrie
Lawnton
Strathpine
Bracken Ridge
Aspley
Stafford
Nundah
BRISBANE AIRPORT

FORT LYTON NP

Tibbeowuccum
Woodford
D'Aguilar
Bracalba
Rocksberg
Ocean View
Moorayfield
Caboolture
Wamuran Basin
Mt Mee
Dayboro
Lake Samsonvale
Closeburn
Mt Samson
Samford Valley
Samford
Ironbark Gully
Ferny Grove
Bellbird Grove
The Gap
Mt Coot-tha
Albany Creek
Enoggera Reservoir

BRISBANE

Kilcoy
Winya
Woodford
Neurum
Villeneuve
Delaneys Creek
Mt Archer
Mt Mee
Mt Pleasant
Mt Byron
Glengariff Wine Estate
The Bulls Knob
BRISBANE FOREST PARK
Wivenhoe Outlook
D'Aguilar Range Scenic Drive
Mt Glorious
MANORINA NP
Mt Lawson
Samford Historical Museum
Jollys Lookout
McAfees Lookout
Camp Mt Lookout
BOOMBANA NP
Westridge Lookout
Mt Nebo
Mt England
Gold Creek Reservoir
Lake Manchester
Enoggera Reservoir

Toogoolawah
Mt Beppo
Caboonbah Homestead
Caboonbah
Murrumba
Mt Esk
ESK
Club Hotel
Mt Brisbane
Somerset Dam
Lake Somerset
Crossdale
Mt Sim Jue
Bryden
Dundas
Cedar Flats
Split Yard Creek Dam
Lake Wivenhoe
Captain Logan Camp
Logan Inlet
Coominya
Wivenhoe Dam
Fig Tree
Fernvale
Lowood
Glamorganvale
Mt Cosby
Moggill
Karalee
Tivoli
Riverview
Dinmore
IPSWICH
Redbank Plains
Browns Plains
Boronia Heights
LOGAN
Slacks Creek
Loganholme
Loganlea
Carbrook

Colinton
Gregors Creek
Hazeldean
Buff Mtn
Mt Sevastopol
Cressbrook Dam
CROWS NEST NP
Ravensbourne
RAVENSBOURNE NP
Perseverance
Mt Perseverance
White Mtn
Buaraba
Bellevue Homestead
Mount Tarampa
Kentville
Atkinsons Lagoon
Prenzlau
Coolana
Tarampa
Minden
Marburg
Woodlands (Historic House)
Haigslea
Amberley
Amberley RAAF Base
Willowbank
Birru Walloon
Rosewood
Calvert
Thagoona
Woodlands (Historic House)

Gallanani
Biarra
Mt Deongwar
Fulham Vale
Mount Beppo
Coominya

Hampton
Iredale
Lilydale
Ma Ma Creek
Mt Whitestone
Upper Tenthill
Grandchester
Blenheim
Ropeley
Tenthill
Woodlands
UQ Gatton
Gatton
Forest Hill
Laidley
Laidley Pioneer Village
Summerholm
Hatton Vale
Mount Tarampa
Balaam Hill
Grantham

VENMAN BUSHLAND NP

REDLAND

Daisy Hill Koala Park
Mt Cotton
Mt Gravatt
Toowong
Kenmore
Jindalee
Acacia Ridge
Darra
Inala
Calamvale
Woodridge
Eight Mile Plains
Coorparoo

Mt Coot-tha

BRISBANE HIGHWAY
WARREGO HIGHWAY
CUNNINGHAM HIGHWAY
D'AGUILAR HIGHWAY
BRISBANE VALLEY
BRISBANE RIVER
LOCKYER CREEK
Bremer River

85
1
17
2
15
1

Things to See and Do

1   Visit Brisbane Forest Park Headquarters to explore the wildlife display and walking track (Ph: 07 3300 4855)

2   Have lunch at Bellbird Grove picnic ground where walks take in old mine shafts and rebuilt Aboriginal huts

3   See the sights from McAfees Lookout

4   Camp Mountain Lookout offers great views across the Samford Valley

5   Jolly's Lookout is best for views to the north and east. Take a walk through dense eucalypt forest (8 km) to Boombana National Park

6   Westridge Lookout, 3 km past Mount Nebo, is a great spot to watch the sky fill with colour when the sun sets

7   Mount Glorious has a café, restaurant, craft cottage, youth camp and picnic area all located near the entrance to the D'Aguilar National Park

Lace Monitor One of the 26 species of goanna in Australia, Lace Monitors can often be seen in the forests and woodlands near Brisbane.

Wonga Pigeon An inhabitant of South-East Queensland's rainforests, vine thickets and eucalypt forests, the Wonga Pigeon is not commonly seen. It forages on the forest floor but may flap into the treetops if threatened.

Exploring the Forest on Foot

Where better to recover from the stresses of city living than in the largest tract of bushland located near an Australian capital city? The 1140 ha **Maiala** section of **D'Aguilar National Park** at Mount Glorious boasts some of Brisbane's closest and most spectacular rainforest walks: the easy 2 km **Maiala Circuit track**, the **Greenes Falls track**, the **Cypress Grove track**, and the **Westside track** that, in places, passes along steep slopes and cliff-tops on the southern side of Mount Glorious.

From the open lawn of the Maiala picnic ground with its majestic bunya and hoop pines, the tracks plunge directly into a fine example of moist, cool, subtropical rainforest. Take the "look up, look around, look down" approach to appreciate this beautiful place. Look up and you'll see the underside of the leafy canopy that protects all below and creates a damp environment for the rainforest plants and wildlife to thrive. Crows nest ferns cling to the trees, vines dangle and tangle, the tall slim trunks of palms reach for the scarce sunlight that filters through the canopy. All around you are the moss- and lichen-covered trunks of giant rainforest trees, dark against the understorey of ferns and young palms. Look down and explore the forest floor where leaf litter and fallen tree trunks are broken down by moisture, ants, insects, fungi and microscopic organisms to provide nourishment for other plants in a cycle of decay and renewal.

As you look up, around and down, be on the lookout for the creatures that call the rainforest home – brush-turkeys, pigeons, parrots, owls, snakes, lizards, frogs, wallabies, possums, bandicoots, native mice and rats, and the myriad invertebrates such as spiders, butterflies and mantids.

A journey through places rich with wildlife won't always reward with sightings of all of the various creatures that live there. You won't see possums in daytime; at night most of the birds will be roosting quietly. But one of the joys of bushwalking is that even if you don't see much of the wildlife in a particular place, you know they are there, sharing their home with you. Respect for their home – and the whole environment – is an important part of the experience that can only be had because such places and all the living things in them are preserved and protected. Not to conserve such places is to abrogate an obligation to our planet. To destroy such places is to diminish our humanity.

A place of peaceful rainforest and majestic eucalypts Maiala has a wonderful variety of natural places to explore. Experience the serenity of rainforest complete with gurgling streams, waterfalls and moss-covered rocks, stroll amongst the giants of open eucalypt forest or experience the whisper of wind in a grove of native Cypress pine.

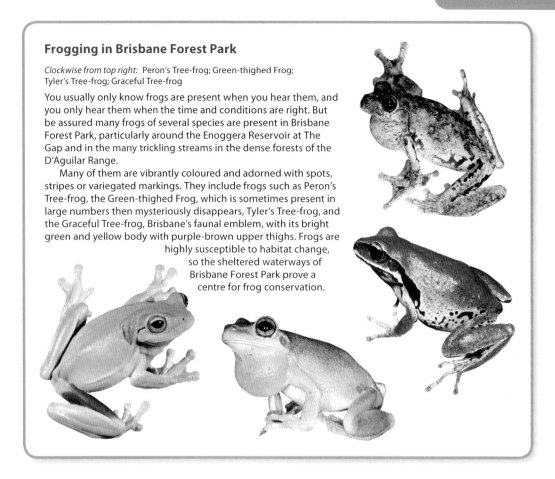

Frogging in Brisbane Forest Park

Clockwise from top right: Peron's Tree-frog; Green-thighed Frog; Tyler's Tree-frog; Graceful Tree-frog

You usually only know frogs are present when you hear them, and you only hear them when the time and conditions are right. But be assured many frogs of several species are present in Brisbane Forest Park, particularly around the Enoggera Reservoir at The Gap and in the many trickling streams in the dense forests of the D'Aguilar Range.

Many of them are vibrantly coloured and adorned with spots, stripes or variegated markings. They include frogs such as Peron's Tree-frog, the Green-thighed Frog, which is sometimes present in large numbers then mysteriously disappears, Tyler's Tree-frog, and the Graceful Tree-frog, Brisbane's faunal emblem, with its bright green and yellow body with purple-brown upper thighs. Frogs are highly susceptible to habitat change, so the sheltered waterways of Brisbane Forest Park prove a centre for frog conservation.

Mount Glorious Walks

Maiala circuit Starting and finishing at the Maiala picnic grounds, where it initially winds 100 m through a grove of hoop pines, this easy 1.9 km walk takes you through typical rainforest. Half buried among the hoop pines is a boiler from a steam engine, a relic once used to drive the saws in a sawmill that operated at Mount Glorious before the area became protected in the early 1900s.

Greenes Falls track This track branches 1 km in both directions from the circuit track to Greenes Falls on Cedar Creek, descending through thick rainforest and ending at a lookout over the falls.

Cypress Grove track A short loop off the Greenes Falls track takes you on a 2.5 km journey on which you'll pass through a grove of native Cypress trees.

Westside track For more adventurous bushwalkers this is a 7 km round trip, but those who prefer to walk just one way can be picked up from an adjoining road. Follow the escarpment west for about 4 km, through rainforest cloaking the southern side of Mount Glorious to the Western Window lookout. The track then traverses steep slopes to end at Lawton Road.

Wivenhoe Outlook Situated 9 km beyond Mount Glorious, this lookout has scenic views over the waters of Lake Wivenhoe and the valleys and wooded hills around the towns of Esk and Toogoolawah.

***Left to right:* Boombana walking track; Greenes Falls; Maiala National Park** Boombana and Maiala are two sections of D'Aguilar National Park which have significant areas of rainforest incorporating a variety of plant life. For those seeking to experience the splendour of the forest while learning about its animal inhabitants and geological formation, guided activities are available in the form of off-track adventure walks, educational activities for children and organised picnics. The park runs an activity program called Go Bush, details of which can be obtained from the Brisbane Forest Park Headquarters.

Lakes Country

The **Brisbane Valley** lies between the D'Aguilar Range and the Great Dividing Range and is a charming region where farms and small towns nestle beside rivers, creeks and forested hills. In this valley you'll find the region's two largest lakes – **Lake Somerset** and **Lake Wivenhoe**. They were formed by damming waterways to provide water and flood mitigation, and are popular with campers, picnickers and devotees of water-sports.

The road west from **Mount Glorious** runs past **The Summit**, the highest point in the D'Aguilar Range, from where it begins its steep descent into the Brisbane Valley near **Wivenhoe Outlook**. From here, the vista of the Brisbane Valley provides a foretaste of the countryside you'll soon be driving through – acres of rolling farmland in the Northbrook Creek valley, off the main river course. Turning left at a T-junction takes you south across the Wivenhoe Dam wall to the Brisbane Valley Highway.

Rainforest Pockets

Amongst thick eucalypt forests are pockets of rainforest rich in plants and wildlife. Tree ferns (*above*) flourish under a canopy that blocks out sunlight, creating a permanently damp understorey of bracken, ferns and palms growing in leaf litter.

Lake Wivenhoe camping Idyllic camping grounds are scattered along the shores of Lake Wivenhoe and Lake Somerset in the Brisbane Valley region. Most are nestled among gum trees between the forest and the water.

Boating and Camping

Lake Wivenhoe has an information centre with history and nature displays. Picnic areas and boat ramps are plentiful along the western shores, with campgrounds at Captain Logan Camp and Lumley Hill. Sailing, canoeing and rowing are popular pastimes made more pleasant by a tranquillity unaffected by power boats, which are banned. The lake draws fishing enthusiasts, who are permitted to use electric-powered boats. **Lake Somerset**, just north of the Lake Wivenhoe backwaters, has picnic and camping facilities near the Somerset Dam and on the lake's western side. Power boating and waterskiing are allowed at Lake Somerset.

Boating on Lake Somerset Waterskiers and boating enthusiasts flock to Lake Somerset, where, unlike Lake Wivenhoe, power boats are allowed. The combination of camping facilities, boat access and clear, deep water makes it a favourite aquatic playground.

Overlooking Lake Wivenhoe from Wivenhoe Outlook in Brisbane Forest Park Just before the descent into the Brisbane Valley after leaving Mount Glorious is Wivenhoe Outlook. From here, the view of the Brisbane Valley to the west is of an expanse of forest and water, but sheltered among the timbered hills and valleys lie farms and pretty towns.

Top to bottom: **Esk Historical Homestead; original Esk Courthouse** Esk Historical Homestead typifies Brisbane Valley residences built on cattle stations during the pioneering era. The courthouse is part of a collection of historic buildings at Caboonbah Homestead near Esk.

Round and About Esk

The jewel of the Brisbane Valley is the elegant little town of Esk. The town's heritage as one of the State's frontier settlements is reflected in its many grand buildings, such as the Heritage-listed **Esk Historical Homestead**, which offers Devonshire tea, and an insight into pioneering days.

Other historic buildings in the Esk region include: **Bellevue Homestead** at Coominya, west of Wivenhoe Dam, which was restored by the National Trust after being relocated when the dam was built; and **St Andrews Church**, built in 1912 at Toogoolawah, 19 km north of Esk, and designed by Australian architect Robin Dods.

Things to See and Do

1　Esk Historical Homestead, 212 Ipswich St, Esk (Ph: 07 5424 2424)

2　Glengarrif Historic Estate and Winery, 3234 Mt Mee Road, Dayboro (Ph: 07 34251299)

3　Caboonbah Homestead, Esk-Somerset Dam Road, Toogoolawah (Ph: 07 5423 1553)

4　Bellevue Homestead, Coominya, Brisbane Valley (Ph: 07 5423 1553)

5　Hay Cottage, Roderick Cruice Park, William St, Dayboro (Ph: 07 3425 1788)

From the heart of the Brisbane Valley at Esk there are two ways of making the return trip to Brisbane: the D'Aguilar Highway to the north or the Warrego Highway to the south. The northern route is perhaps the more interesting, taking you past Lake Somerset to **Kilcoy** where you'll find a park dedicated to the Yowie – the Australian version of the mythical Yeti – said to roam rugged country around the Kilcoy hills. You then travel east to **Woodford**, where the famous **Woodford Folk Festival** is held each December, and to the hamlet of **D'Aguilar** where you turn south through **Mount Mee**, **Dayboro** and **Samford**.

Round and About Dayboro

Between Mount Mee and Dayboro is the **Glengarrif Historic Estate and Winery**, an early 1900s Queenslander housing the Wild Vine Cellar and Restaurant. In Dayboro, nestled in the foothills of the D'Aguilar Range, historic **Hay Cottage** houses an information centre and an outlet for the local arts and crafts. Nearby **Samford Village** boasts a historical museum and a faithfully restored country hall, the **Farmers Hall**, while the bar at the **Golden Valley Hotel** in Samford is a reminder of early days, its walls hung with historical items reflecting the area's dairy farming and timber-getting heritage.

Top to bottom: **Main street in Esk, principal town of the Brisbane Valley; Dayboro arts and crafts; Glengariff Historic Estate, overlooking Dayboro on the road to Mount Mee.**

Ipswich

This is the city that might have been Queensland's capital but instead grew to be a little sister to Brisbane. Yet Ipswich is a city of Queensland firsts: first non-convict settlers; first mine (and miners' strike); first provincial city; first railway line; first reticulated water supply; first defence force unit; first secondary school. On 6 June, 1859, when Queen Victoria signed the Letters Patent declaring Queensland a separate colony from New South Wales, the State's first Governor read the proclamation in Ipswich, having travelled by boat up the **Brisbane and Bremer Rivers**. Today Ipswich is a mature, modern city no longer in the shadow of Brisbane, a vibrant centre for the region to the capital's south-west.

History and Settlement

From 1825 to 1839, while Brisbane was still the convict settlement of Moreton Bay, settlers migrated northward from New South Wales to the **Darling Downs**. A restricted area of 50 miles (80 km) around the penal colony of Moreton Bay meant that Ipswich town was as close as free settlers were allowed to go.

Top to bottom: **Views south and north from the water tower at Denmark Hill Conservation Park** Flinders Peak (*right top*) and Mount Goolman dominate the skyline to the south; northward lie the D'Aguilar Range and the Brisbane Valley.

Colonial buildings This fine example of colonial architecture was built in 1877 for the Bank of Australasia. Today it is a restaurant. The red-brick clock tower in the background is the Ipswich Post Office, one of only three Federation-style post offices in Australia. The clock is still wound by hand daily.

With the Brisbane and Bremer Rivers able to be navigated, Ipswich – then called **Limestone Station** after a convict-operated limeburning works – became a centre of trade and commerce. The settlers established large pastoral runs in the rich country of the **Bremer and Brisbane Valleys** and the area's own industrial revolution came with the discovery of coal. Today's heritage of fine public, private and commercial buildings is a legacy of the pastoral and mining wealth from the colonial era.

Gooloowan Heritage House Built in 1864 by Benjamin Cribb, one of the city's early entrepreneurs, the building has been restored and is still used as a private residence. It is open for special tours which include morning and afternoon teas.

Woodlands, Marburg One of the grand rural homes of the region. Woodlands, 30 km west of Ipswich near Marburg, was used for many years as a respite retreat by the Catholic Church. Today it is a convention and reception centre.

Heritage Homes

Ipswich's coalmining, industrial and pastoral origins are reflected in the variety of its buildings, from the opulent residences of mine owners and managers to simple, tiny workers' cottages. In the inner city, classical 19th-century buildings stand alongside the best of modern architecture. The surrounding towns and countryside are graced with majestic rural homes built by wealthy graziers of the colonial era.

Ipswich is rich in buildings of historical significance, such as the **Courthouse** and **Post Office** in the city centre, **Ipswich Grammar School** (Queensland's first secondary school), the colonial era homes on **Dulwich Hill**, and many two-storey hotels with verandahs decorated with cast-iron-lace railings. Also of historical significance are the convict-era **Lime Kiln remains** at Cunningham's Knoll in Ipswich.

Things to See and Do
1 Demark Hill Conservation Park
2 Lime Kiln remains, Cunningham's Knoll
3 Old Town Hall Museum and Art Gallery, Brisbane St, Ipswich (Ph: 07 3813 9222)
4 Incinerator Theatre, Burley Griffin Dr, Ipswich (Ph: 07 3812 3450)

Heritage homes on Denmark Hill Several fine colonial-era homes can be seen on the crest of Denmark Hill just south of the city centre. Visitors can enjoy the Denmark Hill Conservation Park and climb the 64 steps to the top of a water tower for panoramic views of the city and beyond.

Ipswich and Rail History

In 1865, Ipswich became the starting point of the railways in Queensland when the first line was built to **Grandchester**, then called **Bigges Camp**, 35 km to the west. In 1867 the line was extended to **Toowoomba**, yet it was not until 1876 that Ipswich and Brisbane were linked by rail. As the railway network grew, Ipswich became the centre for building and maintaining the locomotives, carriages and wagons. By the 1960s, Ipswich railway workshops were among the biggest and busiest in Australia and had more than 2500 workers. Today the workshops are a working museum, and the city is on one of the major routes of fast electric suburban and inter-city passenger train services that radiate from Brisbane. The line through Ipswich goes on beyond Toowoomba to the State's south-west, carrying freight and bringing back grain, cattle, wool and coal.

A Rich Heritage
Ipswich has over 2000 Australian Heritage buildings, including the **Old Ipswich Court House**, built in 1859, **St Mary's Catholic Church**, the former **Flour Mill**, the late-Georgian-style **Ginn Cottage** from the 1850s, and the **Ipswich Central Mission** on Ellenborough Street. Also Heritage-listed is the **Soldiers Memorial Hall**, which has social, architectural and historical significance and is listed with the National Trust.

The Workshops Rail Museum

Billed as a "big, loud adventure", The Workshops Rail Museum is a great place to experience the romance of the railways that played a vital part in Queensland's development.

In the days when steam locomotives hauled passengers and freight, Ipswich was a major railways centre and the buildings that are now The Workshops Rail Museum were home to the State's biggest locomotive building and maintenance operation.

The museum retains the sense of yesteryear. Here you will find huge steam locomotives – many of them operational – grand passenger carriages, examples of modern trains, interactive displays and railway workers restoring and maintaining real locomotives and rolling stock.

The Workshops Rail Museum, North Street, North Ipswich, is open 9.30 a.m. – 5 p.m. daily except Christmas Day and Anzac Day morning. Enclosed footwear is required (Ph: 07 3432 5100 for entry fee).

Moreton Bay Islands

Dotted throughout the Bay's blue waters are up to 365 islands, most of them unpopulated and many of them appearing as tiny specks on the shimmering horizon. At the Bay's southern end they become more plentiful. Some, such as **St Helena Island** and the larger islands of **Moreton** and **North Stradbroke** contain national parks.

Top to bottom: Mangrove shoreline; Yachting paradise; Model boats in Wynnum Wading Pool; Picnicking along the shore.

Moreton Bay

The convergence of the great sand islands of **Moreton** and **North Stradbroke** forms a barrier to Pacific Ocean breakers and provides Brisbane with the natural harbour of Moreton Bay. The Bay stretches 125 km from **Bribie Island** to the southernmost tip of **South Stradbroke Island**, and is 30 km across at its widest. Its long, sweeping foreshores feature sandy beaches, rocky headlands, mangroves, tidal sand bars, mudflats, and wetlands. Moreton Bay's relatively shallow waters harbour complex ecosystems, including seagrass beds that nurture Dugong and turtles.

As you drive or walk these islands or cross the water by boat or ferry, the sights, sounds and scents of the Bay fill the senses and restore the spirit.

St Helena Island National Park Queensland's only historic site national park, St Helena, near the mouth of the Brisbane River, was reputed to be the harshest prison in the convict era.

Bramble Bay to Waterloo Bay

The mouth of the Brisbane River lies nearly midway along Moreton Bay's mainland shores with **Brisbane Airport** on the northern side and the **Port of Brisbane** at **Fisherman Islands** on the south. Here are kept what were once Brisbane's dirty little secrets – a sewage treatment plant, oil refineries and other industries that tend to congregate around river mouths.

Yet along the Bay's foreshore are pretty bayside suburbs bordered by well-kept public parks and walking paths, as well as boat ramps and harbours, sandy beaches and headland lookouts.

South of the airport is the highly sought-after real estate of **Manly** and **Wynnum** – both upmarket yet relaxed suburbs that are popular with sailors, as the numerous expensive yachts that are moored in the **Manly Boat Harbour** testify.

Wellington Point, the first major headland south of the Brisbane River, is the southernmost point of **Waterloo Bay** – a bay within Moreton Bay. Here, houses line the waterfront and cling to the hills, facing the north-east for stunning views and cooling breezes fresh off the water. Further to the south is **Raby Bay** and the **Redland Shire**.

Manly Boat Harbour with Manly and Wynnum behind Once mangroves and mudflats, the site of the largest recreational boat harbour on the eastern seaboard is home to the Royal Queensland Yacht Squadron, boating and sailing clubs and the Australian Volunteer Coast Guard.

The city's earliest "seaside" suburbs are located north of the airport, on Bramble Bay: **Nudgee Beach**, **Shorncliffe**, **Sandgate** and **Brighton**. Before cars and highways made travel to the beaches of the Gold and Sunshine Coasts easy, this was where Brisbane people went for seaside holidays and Sunday outings. The area retains the atmosphere of a carefree resort with village-like clusters of shops, modest houses and lovely stretches of foreshore with parks, walkways and broad sandy flats to stroll across at low tide. Many leisure facilities, as well as natural attractions such as Boondall Wetlands environmental reserve, make these places worth a visit.

Boondall Wetlands, just 15 km from the city over the **Gateway Bridge**, provides habitat for a wealth of flora and wildlife. Over 1000 ha are set aside here to preserve open forest, melaleuca swamp, marshes and mangroves that play host to migratory wading birds.

Things to See and Do
1   Ormiston House, Wellington St, Ormiston
2   Boondall Wetlands, 60 Mt Nebo Road, Boondall
3   Redlands Museum, 60 Smith St, Cleveland
4   Eprapah Environmental Centre, Cnr Colburn Ave & Cleveland-Redland Bay Road, Victoria Point.
5   Cleveland Lighthouse, Shore St, Cleveland
6   Point Halloran Conservation Reserve, Orana St, Victoria Point
7   Daisy Hill Koala Centre, Daisy Hill Road, Daisy Hill

Victoria Point with Brisbane in the background Catch the ferry to Coochiemudlo Island, stroll, cycle or roller-blade the esplanade, launch a boat, or picnic, swim and sunbathe.

The Redlands

South of **Wynnum** and **Manly** is **Redlands**, a sprawling area noted and named for its deep-red, rich volcanic soil. The suburbs of **Cleveland**, **Victoria Point** and **Redland Bay** line the Bay's foreshores – and in its more tranquil waters are dozens of smaller islands with **North Stradbroke Island** as their backdrop. Boating and sailing is safer here than in the open waters to the north, and many of the residents on the populated islands commute to the mainland via ferries and water taxis.

The Redlands were once the salad bowl of Brisbane. The red soils for which Redland Bay was named were suited to growing all kinds of fruit and vegetables, particularly strawberries. Farms still dot the area but the spread of suburbia has overtaken many of them. Sugar cane was also once grown in the Redlands and historic **Ormiston House** is a link with the early days of the industry. Captain Louis Hope, a founder of Queensland's sugar industry, had the house built by Scottish craftsmen using bricks made on the property and local cypress pine. **Whepstead Manor** in Wellington Point was built in 1889 by Captain Hope's manager, Gilbert Burnett. Other links with the past, including the old **Cleveland Point Lighthouse** built in 1864, can be found by following the **Cleveland Point Heritage Trail**. Go to www.more2redlands.com.au/more2/explore and click on the links.

The signposted and mapped **Southern Moreton Bay Tourist Drive** (also at the more2redlands website) takes you on a trek through some of the most interesting places in the shire. Starting at the northern end of the Redlands at Wellington Point at the end of Main Road, the first stop is Ormiston House, then on to **Black Swamp Wetlands** and past the old Cleveland Lighthouse at the end of Shore Street. Stop in at the **Redlands Museum** (60 Smith Street) before heading out to Victoria Point where you can visit the **Eprapah Environmental Centre**, the **Point Halloran Conservation Reserve** – home to colonies of Koalas – and the **Egret Colony Wetlands**. Victoria Point is also the ferry departure point for **Coochiemudlo Island**.

In the hinterland, inland from Redland Bay, are the suburbs of **Mt Cotton** and **Daisy Hill**. Much of the bushland between these suburbs and Redland Bay is designated as a "Koala Corridor" – a green strip where eucalypt trees are protected for the preservation of Australia's cuddliest-looking marsupial. The **Daisy Hill Koala Centre** is a sanctuary that provides care for injured Koalas and educates the public about these extraordinary animals (Daisy Hill Road, Daisy Hill, Ph: 07 3299 1032).

Top to bottom: **Coochiemudlo Island; A resident of the Daisy Hill Koala Sanctuary** Coochiemudlo, like many of the southern Bay islands, has safe swimming beaches; Redlands forests are home to colonies of Koalas.

Top to bottom: **Sandgate Marina in Cabbage Tree Creek; Sandgate village; Mural on a Redcliffe public toilet; Scarborough Marina on Deception Bay.**

Redcliffe – Site of Queensland's First Settlement

North of the mouth of the **Pine River**, which flows into **Bramble Bay**, is the Redcliffe peninsula, where Queensland was first settled.

When the British were looking for a new site for a penal colony to take Sydney's most intractable convicts, they sent John Oxley to explore the area that Cook and Flinders had earlier described. On Oxley's recommendation, the brig *Amity* was despatched to Red Cliff Point, arriving in September 1824, but, in less than a year, the place was deemed unsuitable, not least because of the clouds of mosquitoes, and the colony moved to where Brisbane city centre is today.

It was another 40 years before British settlers returned to Redcliffe and, after Brisbane became a free settlement in 1842, farms were established in the area. The settlements have grown into the bayside suburbs of **Clontarf**, **Woody Point**, **Margate**, **Redcliffe** and **Scarborough**.

Redcliffe is a peninsula typified by headlands of red-soil cliffs jutting out into northern Moreton Bay. To the north is **Deception Bay** at the mouth of the **Caboolture River** and, to the south, Bramble Bay at the mouth of the **Pine River**. Between the red headlands lie a 22 km string of sandy, family-friendly beaches which benefit from the safe Moreton Bay swell without the crashing, direct ocean waves.

Redcliffe Pier This redeveloped icon of early Redcliffe is a major visitor attraction.

Shorncliffe Pier Starting point for the annual Brisbane–Gladstone Yacht Race.

Bridging Redcliffe–Brisbane

Until 1935, when the **Hornibrook Bridge** between Brighton and Clontarf was opened, Redcliffe was accessible from Brisbane only by road off the Bruce Highway. The Hornibrook Highway and its successor, the Houghton Highway, spanned the Pine estuary and linked Redcliffe and Brisbane, relieving the area of its isolation from the city.

But the construction of the bridge meant the loss of sea trips between Brisbane, Sandgate and Redcliffe. Vessels such as the *Koopa* and the *Merrimar* carried hundreds of excited daytrippers down the Brisbane River, across the Bay and to the still-existing piers at Sandgate and Redcliffe. Today, increasing traffic has led to plans for yet another bridge across the mouth of the Pine River, while maintaining part of the old hardwood Hornibrook Bridge for fishing and other recreational activities.

Most of Redcliffe's bayside communities are a touch nostalgic, still harbouring the relaxed attitude and innocence that once made them premier seaside resorts. Annual events reflect this sense of seaside charm. Each Easter, Redcliffe holds the **Festival of Sails** on Sutton Beach to coincide with the start of the **Brisbane–Gladstone Yacht Race**. Live music and entertainment, beachside markets and a parachuting Easter Bunny are the main features. In May, the city stages **Kitefest** and thousands of kites take to the skies above Pelican Park, Clontarf.

Each September, Redcliffe's **First Settlement Festival** commemorates Redcliffe's status as Queensland's first European settlement.

Osprey House Environmental Centre in wetlands at Griffin near the mouth of the Pine River.

Boondall Wetlands

Left: Rainbow Bee-eater. *Bottom left:* Lotus Lily. *Bottom right:* Darter or Snake Bird.

Brisbane's largest wetlands, Boondall Wetlands, lie on the northern shore of Moreton Bay between Nudgee Beach and Shorncliffe.

They include more than 1000 ha of tidal flats, mangroves, saltmarshes, melaleuca wetlands, grasslands, open forests and woodlands and are home to an amazing variety of birds, including Black-shouldered Kites, kestrels, ospreys, ducks and kingfishers. The wetlands are also home to frogs, flying foxes, possums, gliders, skinks and lizards.

Boondall Wetlands are part of a chain of coastal wetlands listed under the Ramsar Convention, an international treaty for the conservation and wise use of wetlands, particularly to protect migratory waders.

Aboriginal people lived in this area for a long time and many continue to have links to the land. A totem trail through the wetlands includes 18 aluminium totems that symbolise aspects of their culture, explaining how Aboriginal clans used the area's flora, fauna and land.

The **Boondall Wetlands Environment Centre** has displays and activities that relate to the reserve's environmental and cultural heritage (Ph: 07 3865 5187).

A lookout gives views of the wetlands and Moreton Bay and you can explore the wetlands through the 5-km canoe trail that winds through the reserve.

Bribie Island

Bribie Island, at the north-west corner of Moreton Bay, hugs the mainland coast but is divided from it by **Pumicestone Passage**. Bribie's population centres are concentrated on the southern end of the island; most of the rest is designated the **Bribie Island Recreation Area** that includes **Bribie Island National Park**, the beach to low water mark and other public land. The Glass House Mountains across Pumicestone Passage provide a beautiful backdrop, particularly at sunset. Bribie may not have the presence of Moreton and North Stradbroke Islands, but it has its own charm, fame and history.

The story goes that Bribie Island's name comes from an escaped convict named Bribey (or Brieby) who lived with Aborigines on the island. He was not the first European to live there, nor the only one to live with local Indigenous people. When John Oxley was sent from Sydney in the 1820s to look for a site for a penal colony, he found three of a four-man crew who, on a voyage from Sydney, had been shipwrecked by storms. Bribie Island also came to be home to the internationally renowned artist Ian Fairweather, who became a recluse in the island's bush from 1953 until his death in 1974.

Just 65 km north of Brisbane, Bribie is linked to the mainland by a road bridge. Its surf beach is the closest to Brisbane, and the island is an easily accessible place for bushwalking, beachwalking, swimming, boating and fishing. Beachfront camping and four-wheel-driving on the beach and in some other parts of the Recreation Area are allowed with permits from the Queensland Parks and Wildlife Service. Great numbers of migratory and wading birds in the **Buckley's Hole Conservation Park** on the southern end of the island attract birdwatchers and naturalists.

Left to right: **Sailing on Pumicestone Passage; aerial view of the northern tip of Bribie Island; Sunset over Pumicestone Passage and the Glass House Mountains** Bribie Island is a popular and safe boating bond fishing spot. To the west, across the passage, are the Glass House Mountains, which are a spectacle at sunset and when storms gather over them. The eastern side of Bribie Island has surfing beaches that are also popular with surf anglers.

Moreton Bay Marine Park

Moreton Bay was formed by sand that was swept north on ocean currents and deposited to become the sand islands that form the eastern barrier of the Bay and the Pacific Ocean. Its waters, islands and foreshores are one of the region's most important natural, recreational, cultural and economic assets.

The Bay, protected as a marine park since 1993, remains mostly in its natural state. Its beaches, sandbanks and mudflats are internationally significant as wetland habitats crucial for migratory shorebirds, while its seagrass beds are important grazing grounds for turtles and Dugong. The park covers most of the Bay's tidal lands and seaward waters beyond the east coasts of **Bribie, Moreton, North Stradbroke and South Stradbroke Islands**. Its vast area includes land to the highest astronomical tide and freehold land whose owner has kindly agreed to its inclusion.

Moreton Bay Marine Park is split into five zones plus six designated areas that provide a balance between human needs and the need to conserve the Bay's special natural values. Each zone defines activities that are allowed, those that require permits and those that are prohibited. General use zones, which make up most of the park, allow reasonable use and enjoyment and allow activities such as shipping. Habitat zones exclude activities such as shipping and mining but allow reasonable other uses while maintaining the natural environment. Conservation zones preserve the natural condition to the greatest possible extent and provide for recreational activities free from commercial trawling. Protection zones are "look but don't take" areas of high conservation value where all forms of fishing and extracting are prohibited, allowing people to enjoy the undisturbed nature of the area and ensuring an undisturbed existence for its natural inhabitants. Some areas are designated for special purposes, such as areas where vessels are banned to protect turtles and Dugong.

On littering and pollution, the message is: "Keep Moreton Bay Beautiful" – if you ship it in, ship it out. And there is a message too for the people of the Moreton Bay region: what goes down your stormwater drain, sink and toilet or on your garden may eventually reach the Bay.

Moreton Bay is renowned for its fishing grounds and while fishing activities are largely unaffected by zoning, some restrictions apply to encourage sustainable use.

Above: **Trevally** are one of the numerous species of fish that make Moreton Bay a top fishing locality. *Below:* **Sponge, Tunicate, Anemone and Feather Sea Stars** are marine invertebrates that will often congregate around and attach themselves to a solid object such as a small outcrop of rock.

Dugong and Seagrass

Right: Female Dugong and young. *Below left:* The Porcelain Crab lives commensally (one species assists with the feeding of another) with a sea anemone. These crabs are relatively common in Moreton Bay. *Below right:* Many brightly coloured sea stars live among the sea grasses of Moreton Bay.

Moreton Bay is the only place on earth where turtles and Dugong live so close to a major city. Both animals are slow moving and, although they surface to breathe, they often swim just below the surface feeding in seagrass beds to the north and south of Rous Channel and South Passage between Moreton Island and North Stradbroke Island and on the northern side of Peel Island. These are declared Dugong and turtle "go-slow" areas for boats.

Whales and Dolphins

Above: Bottlenose Dolphins are permanent residents.
Right: Humpback Whales are seasonal visitors to Moreton Bay.

Moreton Bay is often visited by Humpback Whales on their annual winter migration north to the warm Great Barrier Reef waters to breed or on their return to the Southern Ocean with their calves. These peaceful migrations are quite different from the mid-20th century when whales were hunted in southern Queensland waters and butchered at **Tangalooma** on Moreton Island. Today Tangalooma is a resort and, in a further contrast with whaling, Bottlenose Dolphins are a tourist attraction and visitors can interact with these marine mammals. Dolphins are common in most parts of Moreton Bay and can often be seen following boats and ferries.

Reef Stonefish, shown here camouflaged among the algae and encrusting organisms of the Tangalooma Wrecks, are common but often difficult to locate.

Stonefish, even seen against a sandy background, can easily be mistaken for rocks or coral. If stung by a Stonefish, immerse the area in hot water and seek immediate medical advice.

The Bay's Dangerous Marine Life

Moreton Bay, like most marine environments, has its share of dangerous animals and plants. The four pictured are just some of them; others include seasnakes and carnivorous predators such as sharks.

The **Reef Stonefish** is the most venomous fish in the world. Sharp spines located in its dorsal fin inject extremely poisonous venom. There have been no recorded deaths in Australia, thanks to the development of an antivenom, but there have been many recorded stings. The **Blue Ringed Octopus** may look insignificant but this tiny octopus is the world's most dangerous. Just a small amount of the neurotoxin in its saliva can cause paralysis and death – there is currently no antidote.

From left to right: **Textile Coneshell; Lionfish; Ijima's Urchin and Blue Ringed Octopus.**

Moreton Bay's Birds

Left: Egret *Right:* Nankeen Night Heron *Above:* Flocks of migratory birds pass through Moreton Bay.

More than 50,000 migratory shorebirds from 34 species visit the Moreton Bay wetlands each year and the Bay is internationally recognised as an important site for their survival. Every summer, many wading birds feed on the food reserves in the Bay and by April they leave to fly thousands of kilometres to breed in Arctic and sub-Arctic regions. Species of conservation concern include the Beach Stone-curlew, Eastern Curlew, Painted Snipe and Sooty Oystercatcher. More common wading species, such as egrets and herons, can often be seen hunting along the tideline or around mangroves.

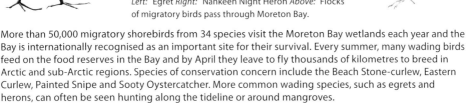

Moreton Island

From almost every eastern vantage point around Brisbane that provides a vista of Moreton Bay, the long, low, dark-green silhouette of Moreton Island can be seen on the horizon. Distinctive white sandblows – **Big Sandhills** and **Little Sandhills** – are located towards the island's southern end, while about half-way along is **Mount Tempest** – the highest sand dune in the world. From its summit, 280 m above sea level, views stretch across the Bay to Brisbane and north-west to the Glass House Mountains. Moreton Island, at almost 40 km long, 9 km wide at the northern end and tapering to **Reeders Point** in the south, is a spectacular summer playground for the residents of South-East Queensland. The island is all sand, except for the rocky **Cape Moreton** area to the north-east, but it is covered in stunted banksia and eucalypt scrub, swampy heathland and bent wind-blown casuarinas that line the pristine beaches. On its coast, stretches

Cape Moreton Lighthouse This convict-built sandstone lighthouse has been a sentinel of Cape Moreton since 1858.

of white sand are met by Pacific Ocean breakers that lap the sunken hulls of shipwrecks, attracting a multitude of coloured fish that delight divers and snorkellers. Towards Cape Moreton, you can also swim in the freshwater **Blue Lagoon**. In a high, narrow valley to the north of Mount Tempest is a patch of forest where tall trees form a shady canopy and vines and ferns grow in the moist leaf litter that carpets the sand floor.

Exploring the Island

Moreton Island is national park, except for the **Tangalooma Wild Dolphin Resort** and the townships of **Kooringal** in the south, **Cowan Cowan** on the western side and **Bulwer** in the north-west. Vehicular and passenger ferries run from Brisbane to Kooringal and Tangalooma, and from Redcliffe to Bulwer. There are two ways to get around Moreton Island: four-wheel-driving or hiking. Many choose to "go bush", hiking and camping to get closer to nature. Both camping and vehicle permits are required and you can buy these from ferry operators. If you choose to drive, vehicles should remain in four-wheel-drive with lowered tyre pressure to avoid getting bogged in the sand. To protect the island's fragile ecosystems, drive only on the designated tracks or on the beach at low tide. The speed limit is 60 km/h and normal road rules apply.

Eastern Beach to Cape Moreton Start at Kooringal and cross east to the ocean side following almost 40 km of surf beach past coloured sand cliffs, tree-covered dunes and freshwater creeks up to Cape Moreton. Halfway along you pass the Tangalooma track and 2 km farther is the Eagers Creek camping area; 5 km on, another track leads to Bulwer and North Point. The next beach exit takes you to Blue Lagoon, a large freshwater lake with a camping area. Onward leads to Cape Moreton, the site of Queensland's oldest lighthouse, built in 1857.

Tangalooma and the Tangalooma Track This track takes you across the island to the eastern beach passing two side tracks – the first to the bare, scrub-surrounded sand dunes of **The Desert** and to the southern beaches and Big and Little Sandhills; the second runs north to the foothills of Mount Tempest. Walk up the mountain trail or follow an old road north along the centre of the island to meet the Bulwer track from the eastern beach.

Top to bottom: **The Big Sandhills; Unloading vehicles from a ferry; Resort living at the Tangalooma Wild Dolphin Resort; Dune surfing** Moreton Island is close to the city of Brisbane but is a world apart, providing a wealth of scenic beauty free from the ugliness of bitumen roads and high-rise buildings.

Diving on Moreton Island

The waters around Moreton Island are crystal clear, with scattered natural and artificial reefs that are perfect for recreational diving. The most popular sites are **Flinders Reef**, **Smith Rock** and **Hutchison Shoal** off the north-eastern corner of the island. Also on the ocean side, but further south, are **Henderson Rock** and **Cherubs Cave**. On the Bay side lie the **Curtin Artificial Reef**, formed by the scuttling of the barge *Amsterdam* near Bulwer, and **The Wrecks** at **Tangalooma**. The wrecks of the *St Paul* and *Cementco* also provide a watery wonderland. On the north-western corner of the island, **Comboyuro Point** is an excellent site for drift diving.

Things to See and Do

1 Feed wild Bottlenose Dolphins

2 Visit Queensland's oldest lighthouse at Cape Moreton

3 Dive or snorkel around the many wrecks

4 Sand toboggan at Big and Little Sandhills

Underwater wonders Moreton Island has a number of natural and artificial reefs frequented by colourful coral and fish, such as the Coral Cod and Squirrelfish shown above. The island's waters are suitable for diving almost year round as water temperature is usually above 17° Celsius.

The **Curtin Artificial Reef**, established by the Underwater Research Group of Queensland in 1968, has 30 wrecks including two former tug boats and gravel barges, plus hundreds of tyres and car bodies. It is used for wreck diving courses, as several wrecks are large enough for safe penetration. The tugs *Melbourne* and *Loevenstein* and the gravel barges *Estrella del Mar* and *Barrambin* are particularly good to explore.

The reef ranges in depth from 14 m to 25 m and is home to a wide assortment of fish – huge Queensland Blue Groper and schools of turrum, trevally and mackerel as well as Coronation Trout, Potato Cod, Blue Angelfish, butterfly fish, kingfish, Red Emperor, bream, whiting, tuskfish, parrots, wrasse and wobbegong sharks.

The 15 hulks at **Tangalooma**, scuttled to form a small craft anchorage in 1963, are an excellent snorkelling and shallow scuba diving site.

Above, top to bottom:
Artificial reef diving The Wrecks at Tangalooma are a popular place for scuba diving and snorkelling; Scuba divers encounter thousands of species of fish, both schooling and solitary, at the island's many dive sites.

The Dolphins of Tangalooma

A close encounter with dolphins in their natural environment is one of the most uplifting experiences for the visitor to **Wild Dolphin Resort** at Tangalooma. Each evening up to a dozen of these beautiful mammals swim up to the floodlit beach near the jetty to enjoy fresh fish thrown by visitors and the resort's dolphin care staff.

The Dolphin Care Program aims to ensure that the dolphins' interaction with humans does not harm the animals in any way or disturb their natural behaviour patterns. Carers restrict the amount of fish given to the dolphins to less than a fifth of their daily requirements so that they still need to hunt and won't become dependent on hand-outs or become too tame. The dolphins are totally wild and untrained. Human contact with them is limited so that they remain wary of people.

Part of the program is to educate the public about dolphins, to broaden understanding and to encourage concern for the future of these magnificent animals.

Oodgeroo Noonuccal

The Aboriginal name for North Stradbroke Island is *Minjerribah* and for many thousands of years the island was home to a large Aboriginal population from the Nunukal, Nughie and Goenpil tribes. It was also home to one of Australia's most celebrated Indigenous poets, Kath Walker, who, in 1988, adopted her traditional name of Oodgeroo Noonuccal, which means "paperbark tree" in her native language. She was the first Aboriginal woman to publish a book and was awarded an MBE in 1970, which she returned in 1988 in protest at the condition of her people.

Frenchmans Bay Waves crash on the beach between Point Lookout and Dune Rocks.

North Stradbroke Island

Easily reached by water taxi or vehicular ferry from Brisbane's bayside, locals call this sand island "Straddie" with the genuine affection reserved for a special place.

North Stradbroke Island is the most accessible and developed of the three great sand islands east of **Moreton Bay**. It has three communities at its northern end – **Dunwich**, **Amity** and **Point Lookout** – all linked by sealed roads. Unlike nearby Moreton Island, Straddie has plenty of holiday accommodation, from resorts and upmarket holiday homes to units, busy backpacker hostels, excellent camping grounds and a hotel.

Point Lookout From this seat, called Cook's Chair, the beach stretches south to Jumpinpin.

Exploring the Island

Unlike the four-wheel-driving zones of Moreton and Fraser Islands, North Stradbroke can be easily explored in a conventional car, with the exception being a track along the beach at the southern end at **Jumpinpin**, where the island was once linked to South Stradbroke Island.

Cylinder Beach One of the most popular beaches and camping places on the island.

Dunwich, Brown Lake and Blue Lake Dunwich, once a convict settlement and quarantine station, is the gateway to the island. You arrive here from the mainland to find a pretty township with a National-Trust-listed cemetery dating from 1847 and a historical museum. Inland, 4 km along Tazi Road, is Brown Lake, a perched lake bounded by paperbarks and banksias, and named for its tea-coloured water – the result of plant tannins seeping into the lake. The road continues across the island through Blue Lake National Park, which surrounds the clear, deep Blue Lake.

Aerial view of Point Lookout One of the more magical spots in South-East Queensland, Point Lookout provides views down Blue Lake Beach to the south. It has an equally spectacular outlook to the north-west around Cylinder Beach (*foreground*), Flinders Beach and north to Moreton Island.

Perched Lakes

Top to bottom: Brown Lake; Eastern snake-necked turtle.

North Stradbroke Island has several freshwater lakes but only one of them – **Brown Lake** near Dunwich – is easily accessible. **Blue Lake** in **Blue Lake National Park** is closed to visitors and most other lakes and swamps are set amongst inaccessible scrub.

Brown Lake is a "perched lake": a lake that sits high in sand dunes with its bottom made watertight by plant matter. Tannin in the leaves, bark and twigs that fall into the lake gives the water a sepia "tea" colour. As it is set below the island's water table, nearby Blue Lake is a "window lake" with steep sides and a depth of almost 10 m in places.

North Stradbroke's lakes and swamps and their surrounding bushlands are home to a variety of wildlife, including snakes, turtles, frogs, fish, Eastern Grey Kangaroos and many species of birds. One of the major swamps is Eighteen Mile Swamp, which runs down most of the southern half of the island to Swan Bay. A local legend is that the wreck of a Spanish galleon lies hidden in the swamp, although no sightings have been claimed since the 1970s.

Myora and Myora Springs Just north of Dunwich on the bitumen road to Point Lookout is Myora – the Aboriginal word for meeting place – where you'll find a flora reserve and conservation park. Further on is **Myora Springs Environmental Park** where fresh water flows from springs in Capembah Creek. The forest surrounding the springs abounds with wildlife and the water teems with freshwater crayfish and prawns. A place of great Indigenous importance, Myora contains Aboriginal middens – piles of shells left over from ceremonial feasts. It was also home to the poet Oodgeroo Noonuccal.

Point Lookout This rocky headland that dominates the State's most easterly point was the first place in Queensland named by Captain James Cook on his voyage past in 1770. Today the hills behind Point Lookout and along **Cylinder Beach**, to its west, have become the island's main residential, commercial and tourist centre. The headland at Point Lookout is an ideal place to watch Humpback Whales breaching and splashing on their northward winter migration, or simply to enjoy the inspiring view and the waves crashing on the rocks below.

Blue Lake Beach Access by four-wheel-drive to this 32-km surf beach is from the southern side of Point Lookout or from Tazi Road across the island from Dunwich.

Left to right: **Soldier Crabs; Eastern Grey Kangaroo; Banksia** North Stradbroke Island is a wonderful natural place despite the effects of humans, including extensive sand mining. Its beaches and surrounding waters are largely untouched and nurture Dugong, turtles, fish, crabs, sharks, manta rays and whales. Mammals, reptiles and birdlife thrive in the island's eucalypt forest, scrub and swamp habitats.

North of Brisbane

To the north of Brisbane is a superb region, 200 km from north to south, of beaches, forests, national parks, mountains, farms, towns, cities – and a great island, the biggest sand island on earth. Here, for thousands of years before European settlement, Aborigines lived well on the abundant plants and wildlife of the region.

Australian Pelican

The rich mythology that accompanies many natural attractions to Brisbane's north is testament to their custodianship.

Here are places of astounding natural beauty, some small and tranquil, like a lake nestling behind sand dunes or a secluded beach, others both massive and impressive, such as the Glass House Mountains or the towering forests and coloured sands of Cooloola. Today, many human-created attractions also await visitors to the region. As well as the glitz and glamour of resorts and tourist attractions – and there are plenty of them – are the tiny towns and charming villages of the Conondale and Blackall Ranges. The entire Sunshine Coast, serviced by the Bruce Highway, is crisscrossed by winding minor roads that allow you to fully explore the region.

Heritage and History

The rich soils and rolling hills to Brisbane's north, along with the warm subtropical climate, proved perfect for farming and the area's expansion and settlement owed much to pastoral pursuits. European exploration began in the 1840s and settlers soon followed, trying their hand at dairy farming or fruit-growing. Further north, the flourishing sugar cane industry, followed by gold rushes in the latter half of the 19th century, created much of the region's wealth.

Fraser Island This great sand island is unique and justifiably famous for its coloured sand cliffs.

Towns and Beaches

Hugging the wide, snow-white beaches and jutting headlands of this ever-changing landscape are small holiday resorts and cosmopolitan seaside towns. On the coastal plains and in the hinterland are towns and villages that were once centres for farming communities. Today many are tourism orientated with a myriad of things for the holidaying visitor to see and do.

Conondale Forest In the majestic hinterland mountains thrive eucalypt forests and rainforests that are excellent for bushwalking.

Mountains and Forests

The region's violent, volcanic prehistory combined with a wet subtropical climate have produced a lush landscape punctuated by mountains – giving rise to diverse ecosystems that foster wildlife. National parks and reserves are easily accessible, and you can watch wildlife in its natural environment, be it scrub-covered headlands or in tall eucalypt forests where bellbirds complement the music of cascading mountain streams.

Top to bottom: **Coolum; Mt Beerwah; Maryborough; Hastings St, Noosa** The region to Brisbane's north, whether coastal or inland, has much appeal.

Heritage Towns

North of the Sunshine Coast the Bruce Highway leads to **Gympie**, a city with a heritage in gold, before heading on to **Maryborough** and **Hervey Bay**, where Fraser Island lies across the Great Sandy Strait. Towns are more sparsely situated in the northern end of the region and a little less touristy. Although the once small seaside villages on Hervey Bay's shores are now virtually a single city, many of the region's tiny towns retain a charming appeal. Further to the north is **Bundaberg**, a major sugar-producing town that is home to one of Australia's most recognisable and potent brews – Bundaberg Rum. It is also the southernmost gateway to the Great Barrier Reef and a departure point for the Southern Reef Islands.

Above: **Bundaberg** A self-guided walking tour along the Heritage City Walk takes visitors past 28 heritage sites in Bundaberg. *Below:* **Fraser Island**, seen from the air is an emerald swathe of land ringed with beaches and sapphire blue waters.

Further Information

Naturally Queensland Information Centre
Ground Flr, 160 Ann St, Brisbane
(Ph: 07 3227 8185)

Tourism Noosa Information Centre
Hasting Street Roundabout, Noosa Heads
(Ph: 07 5547 4988)

Cooloola Region Visitors Information Centre
Dept of Environment and Heritage Building, Lake Alford, Bruce Hwy, Gympie
(Ph: 07 5482 5444)

Maryborough Information Centre
30 Ferry St, Maryborough
(Ph: 07 4121 4111)

Mon Repos Conservation Park

Right: Loggerhead Turtle

Just 15 km north-east of Bundaberg is the Mon Repos Conservation Park, a sanctuary for Loggerhead Turtles, which come to nest along the beaches. Mon Repos is one of the largest rookeries for Loggerhead Turtles in the South Pacific and thousands of visitors per year experience night-time guided tours to learn more about these endangered marine giants.

Loggerhead Turtles live on coral reefs, and in bays and estuaries off the coast of Queensland, the Northern Territory, Western Australia and New South Wales. They feed on crustaceans, sea jellies and sea urchins and begin their mating cycle in October. From mid-November to February, female turtles may be seen laying their eggs into shallow nests on the beaches. From mid-January until late March, tiny hatchlings leave their nests by the light of the moon and struggle to the water. Only a small percentage of hatchlings survive the arduous journey and even fewer survive to adulthood. Bookings for guided tours are essential and can be made through the **Coral Coast Visitor Information Centre** (Ph: 07 4153 8888).

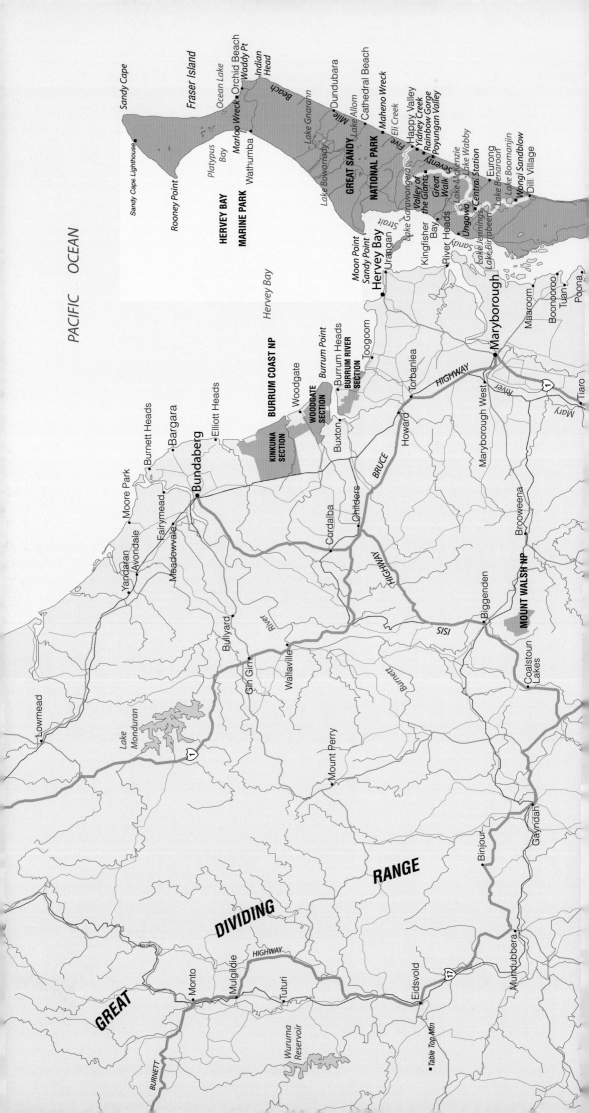

What's in a Name?

When James Cook sailed past in 1770, he noted that the cluster of mountains on the South-East Queensland hinterland resembled the glass houses in Yorkshire and named them the Glass House Mountains. He was referring to large conical furnaces used to make glass, not glass houses where plants are grown. Smoke from fires lit by Aborigines looked like the smoke from the furnace fires.

Top to bottom: **Mount Beerwah; Mount Coonowrin; Mount Tibrogargan.**

Glass House Mountains

The volcanic plugs of the Glass House Mountains rise majestically above the countryside north of Brisbane like giant stone sentinels, their great age contrasting with the precise rows of nearby pine plantations that have replaced native forests. The mountains are the remnant cores of volcanoes that spewed out lava to form the surrounding ranges 25 million years ago. Once liquid rock, today they are ancient, solid symbols of a past era. Nearest the Bruce Highway is **Tibrogargan**, an imposing 364 m mountain with a great vertical eastern face. To the north-west, serving as a spectacular backdrop, are **Beerwah** – the highest mountain at 556 m – and **Coonowrin** (Crookneck), a spectacular 377-m knife blade of bare basalt. South of Tibrogargan is **Beerburrum**, 278 m, and to the south-west is **Tibberoowuccum**, a tree-covered 220-m hill, and **Tunbubudla** (The Twins) at 296 m and 338 m respectively. Also part of this group are **Ngungun**, 236 m, **Miketeebumulgrai**, 199 m and **Elimbah**, 129 m.

An Aboriginal legend of the origin of the Glass House Mountains tells of a family who were forced to flee as the sea flooded and rose. As they fled, the father, Tibrogargan, asked his eldest son Coonowrin to assist his mother, Beerwah, who was pregnant. But Coonowrin left his mother and ran off to save himself. An angry Tibrogargan struck Coonowrin a heavy blow, which dislocated his neck. Ashamed by his son's cowardice, Tibrogargan turned his back on him and wept. Today, Tibrogargan still faces away from Coonowrin, his tears flowing as mountain streams. Coonowrin's neck is crooked and Beerwah is still heavy with child.

Glass House Mountains National Park

Nine of the 16 mountains collectively known as the Glass House Mountains are national park. The 920-ha Glass House Mountains National Park is divided into five sections among the State forests and farmland. Mountains protected include Beerwah, Tibrogargan, Ngungun and Coonowrin.

Geologically the mountains are two types of rock – trachyte and rhyolite. Vertical columns, formed as the molten rock cooled, can be seen on Mount Beerwah and Mount Coonowrin. Mount Coonowrin is currently closed to the public because of the danger of rock falls, but Beerwah, Tibrogargan and Mount Ngungun have a variety of walking tracks. The 2.6-km return trip to the summit of Mount Beerwah takes up to four hours. The climb is recommended for experienced climbers only, but the 360-degree view from the top is spectacular – north over Maleny, east to Caloundra, south to Brisbane and west to the ranges towards Kingaroy. Tibrogargan's 3-km summit walk is also for experienced climbers and presents similar views. Mount Ngungun, 253 m, has a 700-m moderate grade walk to its summit. The track is steep in places, requiring care where it passes close to cliffs.

Although great swathes of the original forests of the area were cleared for farms or plantation forests, areas of significant native forest are protected in the national park's various sections. They are mainly eucalypt open forest and woodlands containing tall blackbutt and scribbly gum, banksia, she-oak and grass-trees. High on the mountain summits are rare and threatened heath species. Birds seen in most parts of the park include kookaburras, Sulphur-crested Cockatoos, Rainbow Lorikeets and Pale-headed Rosellas. You can also expect to see Koalas, goannas, echidnas, and Eastern Grey Kangaroos throughout the Glass House Mountains region.

The Glass House Mountains seen from Mary Cairncross Road lookout at Maleny This accessible lookout offers a spectacular view of the mountains standing out above the hinterland below.
1. Mt Tibrogargan (364 m); **2. Mt Tibberoowuccum** (220 m); **3. Mt Coonowrin** (377 m); **4. Tunbubudla (The Twins)** (338 m & 296 m); **5. Mt Beerwah** (556 m).

Scenic Drive

The countryside of the Glass House Mountains is crisscrossed with roads, giving visitors a number of ways to get close enough to admire the mountains and, where permitted, climb them.

Sticking to the Bruce Highway gives access only to **Wild Horse Mountain Lookout**, on the eastern side of the highway about halfway between the **Beerburrum** and **Beerwah** turn-offs. Here you'll get a big-picture view of the Glass House Mountains and the ranges beyond. But if you leave the highway at **Caboolture** or **Beerburrum**, you can enjoy a more leisurely trip along the old highway, now called Glass House Mountains Road. This passes the **Matthew Flinders Park** roadside stop and the townships of Beerburrum, **Glasshouse Mountains** and Beerwah.

If you're feeling even more adventurous, explore the back roads to the west of Glass House Mountain Road to see the mountains up close and from many angles. A day-long trip adds to the experience, catching the mountains' many moods as the light changes. Another option is to leave Glass House Mountains Road at the township of Glasshouse Mountains and head west towards **Woodford**. The Glass House–Woodford Road takes you to **Glass House Mountain Lookout** – a picnic spot on an open rise with a view of the mountains and beyond. For a close encounter with Mount Beerwah and Mount Coonowrin, take Mount Beerwah Road off Old Gympie Road. This road runs between these two spectacular mountains to a picnic area on the northern side of Mount Beerwah where a walking track to the summit begins.

Top to bottom: **Mount Beerwah with Mount Coonowrin beyond; Glass House Mountains Lookout** From this lookout you can drive on to Woodford, returning on the northern side of the mountains via Peachester, passing the site of the annual Woodford Folk Festival.

Theme Parks

One of the top attractions of the area is Steve Irwin's **Australia Zoo** (Glass House Mountains Tourist Drive, Beerwah, 9 a.m.–4.30 p.m. daily, Ph: 07 5436 2000 for entry fee). This award-winning park is a fair dinkum Aussie wildlife adventure. Landscaped lakes and gardens are alive with animals and birds. Crocodiles are the showpiece, with feeding and demonstration shows in the Crocoseum, but exotic animals are also covered with tigers and cheetahs in the Tiger Temple.

The **Australian Teamsters Hall Of Fame** and **Spirit of Cobb & Co Museum** (Cnr Old Gympie Rd and Mt Beerwah Rd, Glass House Mountains, Ph: 07 5496 9588 for entry fee) is a tribute to the tradition, people, and way of life in the era of bullock wagons and horse-drawn coaches. Visitors can see carriages being built and repaired, watch wheelwrighting and blacksmithing, ride in an original Cobb & Co coach and enjoy billy tea and damper.

Australia Zoo At Australia Zoo, handlers thrill crowds as they get up close to crocodiles. The displays are held daily at noon in the 5000-seat Animal Planet Crocoseum.

Sunshine Coast – Caloundra to Maroochydore

Around 50 years ago, when the strip of coast from Caloundra to Noosa was little more than scattered seaside holiday towns, the name Sunshine Coast was coined to describe the region blessed with some of Australia's finest beaches. Where once windswept frontal dunes created a barrier between the sea and the paperbark swamps and heathland, today exists a string of thriving resort towns that are rapidly developing into a major centre built on surf and sunshine.

Caloundra

The beaches of Caloundra – **Kings**, **Shelly**, **Moffat** and **Dicky** – are a playground for bodysurfers, bathers and board riders. These beaches, divided

Moffat Beach, Caloundra Running north from the cliffs of Moffat Head, this beach has barbecue areas and picnic tables on its foreshore and is popular with families and anglers.

by rocky headlands, are some of the best surf beaches close to Brisbane. Caloundra, the Sunshine Coast's southern gateway, is a vibrant, modern resort city, its beachfronts lined with apartment blocks and resort complexes that offer high-class accommodation. Restaurants and cafés are plentiful, many offering alfresco dining to make the most of the sunshine and ocean ambience. Caloundra also has fine recreation facilities, parks, bikeways and walking trails. There are several world-class golf courses and one of Queensland's best provincial horse-racing venues, **Corbould Park** (170 Pierce Avenue, Caloundra, Ph: 07 5491 6788). **Caloundra Aerodrome** is home to the **Queensland Air Museum** (Pathfinder Dr, Caloundra; 10 a.m.– 4 p.m. Ph: 07 54925930 for entry fee) with a collection of more than 20 military and civilian aircraft. Jetties and boat ramps are provided for boaters.

Top to bottom: **Caloundra; Mooloolaba; Maroochydore** Caloundra, once a small seaside holiday village, is today one of Queensland's major resort towns, with holiday apartments clustered on its headlands and around its sandy beaches. Mooloolaba is part of the Sunshine Coast's central region. Its harbour is a focus of boating activity and it has beachfront resorts and UnderWater World. Maroochydore, on the picturesque Maroochy River mouth, has one of the area's largest shopping centres, Sunshine Plaza, and 10 km of beach running south to Alexandra Headland.

Mooloolaba

The rocky headland of Point Cartwright, across the Mooloolah River to Mooloolaba's east, protects the river mouth and the city's north-facing beach and esplanade – creating an ideal natural harbour that is sheltered from the south-easterly winds. This also makes the harbour, along with its extensive marina, yacht club, fisheries base and the Sunshine Coast's main coast guard station, a perfect destination for the annual Sydney–Mooloolaba yacht race.

The Wharf, just upstream from the boating facilities, also has a marina and is the site of Mooloolaba's premier attraction, UnderWater World.

The Mooloolaba esplanade, lined with Norfolk Island pines, runs between the beach and a line of medium-rise holiday apartments that face northward giving views up the coast towards Noosa.

Mooloolaba Wharf Yachts sway on the tide in the marina. The wharf is part of the UnderWater World complex and is also home to a number of nightclubs and fashionable shops and restaurants.

Lighthouses
The Sunshine Coast's two lighthouses, at Caloundra and Point Cartwright, are part of a protective string of night lights along the Queensland coast. Others include Cape Moreton on Moreton Island, Double Island Point north of Noosa and Breaksea Spit on the northern end of Fraser Island.

Mooloolaba Beach One of the Sunshine Coast's few beaches with a northerly aspect, the beach is protected by Point Cartwright (*background*).

UnderWater World

Above, left to right: The entrance to UnderWater World; Visitors can get close to seals and other marine creatures.

The fascinating world beneath the waves and at the water's edge can be experienced at Mooloolaba's UnderWater World. From the surface world of billabongs, rock pools and coves complete with seals and otters, you journey in a transparent tunnel to the ocean depths of the 2.5-million-litre Oceanarium. Visitors can also scuba dive with more than 30 sharks in the shark tank. UnderWater World is at The Wharf, Parkyn Parade, Mooloolaba. Ph: 07 5444 8488 for entry fee. Open 9 a.m.– 6 p.m. daily.

Maroochydore

This resort town has the best of both worlds – a fine ocean beach that almost always has good surf and a broad river that is ideal for boating, sailing, fishing and swimming. The **Maroochy River** rises in the ranges of the hinterland, winds across the coastal plain and turns into a broad tidal estuary with mangrove-covered islands, channels, sand spits and banks. Holidaymakers have the choice of riverfront or ocean-front living, with both having medium-rise and high-rise apartments and restaurants, cafés and shops along esplanades and boardwalks.

One of Maroochydore's most popular places is **Cotton Tree**. This riverfront area near the Maroochy River mouth on the southern side is a place of parkland, sandy river edge and safe swimming. Each Sunday morning, craft markets in Main Street offer eclectic and varied wares.

For history buffs, the **Maroochy River Resort** (David Low Way, Maroochy River, Ph; 07 5476 8391) has a lagoon on which floats a two-thirds sized replica of Captain Cook's vessel the *Endeavour*. Also here is the award-winning **Nostalgia Town** (596 David Low Way, Pacific Paradise, Ph: 07 5448 7155), a theme park and souvenir shop that bills itself as "A laugh at the past" and includes an 1863 steam train which ventures through a dinosaur swamp and an enchanted tunnel. The central Sunshine Coast is also a focus of recreational diving – the former Royal Australian Navy destroyer *Brisbane* was recently sunk as a dive wreck.

Sailing on Maroochy River
The river is a popular sailing and boating place.

Surfing the Sunshine Coast Board riders flock to the Coast's beaches all year round.

Sunshine Beach is tucked up against the headland section of Noosa National Park.

Sunshine Coast – Coolum to Noosa NP

North of the Maroochy River a string of beaches run up the coast to Noosa – **Mudjimba**, **Marcoola**, **Yaroomba**, **Coolum**, **Peregian**, **Marcus**, **Sunrise** and **Sunshine**. Extensive areas on the northern side of the river are preserved as the **Maroochy River Conservation Park**, which follows about 4 km of riverside mangrove and paperbark scrub and includes an isthmus and sand spit that form the northern side of the river mouth. Three islands in the river – **Chambers**, **Channel** and **Goat** – are part of the park, which is a refuge for wildlife, particularly seabirds. Just north of the river is **Mount Coolum**, a northern Sunshine Coast landmark. This basalt massif sits close to the shore and is surrounded by national park. A walking track runs to its 207-m summit where the panoramic vista takes in beaches to the north and south, the expanse of the Pacific Ocean and the Glass House Mountains and the Blackall Range to the west. The Maroochy River to Mount Coolum area also has the **Sunshine Coast Airport** – a hub for sightseeing flights as far away as Fraser Island – and two major resort complexes, Twin Waters and Hyatt Regency Coolum. Both have championship golf courses. Up the Maroochy River at **Bli Bli** is a major wetland sanctuary preserved among low coastal land that has been cleared for cane farming.

Coolum Beach is one of the most popular in the northern Sunshine Coast area.

Coolum Beach

A string of rocky headlands at **Point Arkwright** separates **Yaroomba Beach** from Coolum Beach and beaches up to Noosa Head, the area's other distinctive landmark. Coolum Beach usually has good surf and is patrolled in the summer months. Coolum was once a sleepy fishing village and although it is now a sophisticated seaside resort, anglers still appreciate a good catch around the rocks surrounding **Sheltered Cove** and **Point Perry**.

Second Bay, Coolum Colourful rocky headlands and foreshores at Point Arkwright.

Noosa Head and National Park

The forested headland with Noosa Head at its north-east extremity is the jewel of the 477-ha **Noosa National Park**. But the park, which stretches from Coolum up to **Granite Bay**, also contains delicate, low coastal heath and swamp, coastal dunes, creeks and lakes. It is the largest undisturbed rocky coastline and the largest wallum heath remnant close to Brisbane.

The southern parts of the national park include wallum scrub west of **Coolum**, **Peregian**, **Sunshine** and **Sunrise** beaches, and heathland and woodland around **Lake Wyeba** – a shallow saltwater lake that is part of the Noosa River system. On the beach side of the road between Coolum and Peregian is a section of park with significant casuarina- and banksia-covered dunes and swamps and ponds. A narrower beachfront strip runs from Peregian to **Marcus Beach**. These lower parts of the park have complex, delicate ecosystems that are home to many varieties of birds and animals.

Noosa Headland

At the southern end of Noosa's glitzy **Hastings Street** you enter the natural wonderland of the **Noosa National Park**, a place of rainforest and high open heathland with views over ocean and beach of rocky cliffs pummelled by waves, or quiet coves and bays with secluded beaches.

Walking trails take you to picnic spots overlooking **Laguna Bay**, the **Noosa River**, **Noosa Lakes** and the **Cooloola** sandmass, through dense rainforest and then heathland to the cliffs above **Granite Bay**, **Noosa Head** and **Hell's Gates**, and down to the beach of **Alexandra Bay**.

Palm Grove Circuit This is an easy 1-km circuit near the park entrance through rainforest with hoop pines and picabeen palms.

Granite Bay on the northern side of the Noosa headland is one of several pretty bays accessible by foot through the Noosa National Park.

Guardians of the Sands

The rocky headlands along the Southern Queensland coasts and islands are the bulwarks that hold the sands which make up beaches, dunes and coastal plains.

These headlands – such as Point Danger, Burleigh Head, Point Lookout, Cape Moreton, Noosa Head, Double Island Point and Indian Head – are natural groynes. For millions of years, as they still do today, they have trapped the sands that are eroded from Australia's east coast highlands and moved northward by the Eastern Australian Current.

Above: **Noosa Head in Noosa National Park** This great headland area is a natural place close to Noosa's seaside suburbia.

Tanglewood Track An 8.4-km meander through rainforest and open eucalypt woodland to Noosa Head and Hell's Gates. Return via the Coastal Track or Tanglewood Track.

Noosa Hill Track A 3.4-km circuit walk to the highest point on the headland. Views are limited by thick forest.

Coastal Track An easy 5.4-km return walk to Noosa Head along the northern cliff with views of Tea Tree Bay.

Alexandra Bay Take the Tanglewood Track to this secluded bay.

Noosa National Park

Left: Koala spotting is a favourite pastime at Noosa national Park. *Right:* A beautiful old strangler fig on Noosa Headland.

The Noosa region has 60 different ecosystems with more than 1400 species of plants, many of them protected in Noosa National Park. The park's ecosystems range from wallum swamp to mountain rainforest, and contain diverse plant and animal species, many of them rare and threatened, such as the Glossy Black Cockatoo, Red Goshawk, Koala, Swamp Orchid and Christmas Bell. Common animals include wallabies, echidnas and many kinds of snakes and lizards. Birds include many species of seabirds, waterbirds, finches and honeyeaters as well as the White-bellied Sea-Eagle and the Osprey.

Sunshine Coast – Noosa and Tewantin

European Exploration

Surprisingly, this pretty area of the coast was overlooked for settlement until 1870, when Tewantin became a port for the nearby Gympie goldfields. Europeans first explored the coast in 1842, when a notorious escaped Moreton Bay convict known as "Wandi" to the Noosa Aborigines with whom he lived, accompanied Henry Russell Petrie on an expedition to the area.

The **Noosa River** is the dividing line between urban development and largely untouched wilderness. It snakes south to Tewantin, Noosaville and Noosa Heads (usually just called Noosa); and north into **Lakes Cooroibah, Cootharaba and Cooloola** before running almost the entire length of the **Great Sandy National Park**. The park, which includes **Cooloola** and **Fraser Island**, is an immense 54,000-ha area of wilderness where birdlife, wildlife and plantlife flourish. Of the region's cities, **Noosa**, on **Laguna Bay**, is the showpiece and is imbued with an aura of first class. It is a small, cosmopolitan community tucked up against the western side of **Noosa Head**, which protects it from the easterly and south-easterly winds but channels in the north-easterly winds across the bay. **Noosaville** is westward along the Noosa River with delightful parks facing the wide, tidal river and the treed north shore that contains the southern section of the Great Sandy National Park. Further up the river is **Tewantin**, the administrative centre of the area.

Noosa Beach at sunrise Laguna Bay is gilt with the magic of the rising sun over Noosa Head on the horizon.

Beaches

Noosa's **Main Beach** has a worldwide reputation as one of Australia's top tourist destinations. It is a small beach with white sand and good surf when the north-easterlys blow. When high tides erode the sand, more sand is pumped in to replenish the beach. The short beachfront is lined with reputable restaurants, resorts and shops on what is arguably some of the most expensive property in Australia.

Parrots on the beach Casuarinas line Noosa's walkways and attract Rainbow Lorikeets.

Noosa River

The Noosa River rises many kilometres to the north in the rainforests high on the Cooloola sandmass and, as it meets the paperbark scrubs of the coastal lowlands, it forms many channels, creating an Australian version of the Florida Everglades. Here, on the river's more serene stretches, trees overhang the narrow channels of water tinted dark by decaying leaves and moss trails from low branches to brush you as you glide past in a canoe.

The everglades flow into a string of shallow tidal lakes lined with paperbarks, banksias and mangroves. The largest of these is **Lake Cootharaba**, which has lakeside camping and accommodation facilities at **Boreen Point** and is the starting point for visits to the everglades.

Left, top to bottom: **Noosa Beach; Laguna Lookout over Noosa and the Noosa River; Boardwalk in Noosa; Sailing from Noosa Beach; Noosa River near Tewantin** This wide, tidal river is a popular place for boating and fishing. River cruises run upriver to lakes and everglades.

Galleries and Shops

Noosa's **Hastings Street** is one of the best known addresses in Australia. Once little more than a surf club, a few beachside shops, some holiday flats and a caravan park, the street today is as good a place to shop and eat as any in Brisbane, Sydney or Melbourne.

Hastings Street runs parallel to the beach and only about 30 m from the sand. One end is **Noosa National Park**, the other parkland and the river. This 750-m long street is packed with quality restaurants, cafés, boutiques, galleries and gift shops plus the five-star Sheraton Noosa Hotel and other superb hotels and apartments.

The street has been landscaped with trees and potted plants, making it a shady place to stroll and take in the relaxed, holiday atmosphere.

***Top and bottom:* World-class shopping on Hastings Street** This short street just a few metres from the surf of Main Beach has boutiques and galleries with designer clothing and interesting arts and crafts.

Fun in the Sun

Noosa is a holiday playground all year round, a place for international visitors to discover, southerners to holiday and Queenslanders to enjoy the summer heat.

It is also a place of annual festivals. Celebrating the natural wonders of the region is the **Wildflower Weekend** in August. The **Noosa Long Weekend**, in June, is a time to immerse yourself in music, art and theatre. September is **Jazz Festival** time. Also not to be missed is the **Festival of Food** when Noosa's many top restaurants showcase their delectable cuisine.

Noosa Beach, Hastings St and Noosa Heads The holiday playground of the Sunshine Coast.

Fine Dining

The dedicated diner will find Noosa a gourmet smorgasbord. Crammed into **Hastings Street** are dozens of restaurants and cafés offering a variety of cuisines from around the world. The atmosphere is tranquil and relaxed, as befits a holiday town. Most restaurants have outdoor settings or are open to the street or ocean, making the most of the cool sea breezes and the scent of subtropical flowers. Decor, food and service are meticulously first-class, but the informality of casual "beach" dress lends an "all the time in the world" air to alfresco dining.

International cuisine on Hastings Street Dining enhanced by the sight and sound of the surf.

Restaurants on the surf side of the street have the advantage of beachside dining. Some tables are just metres from the sand and you dine to the sound of the breaking waves. At sunset or when the moon is over the water, the dining experience becomes even more memorable.

Sunshine Coast Hinterland

The high country of the Sunshine Coast hinterland is in stark contrast to the beaches and coastal lowlands. Up on the **Blackall Range** you'll find rolling, grassy hills long ago cleared of native forests for farming. In the rougher terrain and plunging valleys are great stands of majestic eucalypts and dense rainforest. This variety of natural and altered landscapes makes tripping through this pretty countryside rewarding. The region is dotted with charming country towns – **Palmwoods**, **Maleny**, **Montville**, **Mapleton** and **Flaxton** on the Blackall Range and **Conondale** and **Kenilworth** to the west towards the Conondale Range. Several national parks and State forests are watered by rocky mountain streams harbouring rare and endangered frogs and crayfish. Through these green spaces winds the track of the **Sunshine Coast Hinterland Great Walk**.

Maleny, the largest of the Blackall Range towns, is close to the southern escarpment north of the Glass House Mountains.

Maleny

This delightful country town, once the centre of an extensive dairy industry but now a mix of town and rural living and tourism, sits on the southern end of the Blackall Range near the head of the **Obi Obi Creek**, which winds down past Kenilworth to join the **Mary River**. Cool mountain air, undulating green hills and patches of surrounding rainforest with views to the Glass House Mountains and the Sunshine Coast make it perfect for a Sunday scenic drive. Stop in town to visit the numerous art and craft galleries, shops selling local produce, restaurants, cafés, guest houses, cottages, cabins and a winery. Maleny also has a **Scarecrow Festival** each September and **Festival of Colour** in November.

Glass House Mountains seen from Mountain View Road, Maleny Elevated towns in the region such as Maleny and Mapleton offer panoramic views of the surrounding attractions. Here, the three largest peaks of the Glass House Mountains, from left, Mount Tibrogargan, Mount Coonowrin and Mount Beerwah, rise from the emerald plains of the Hinterland.

Visitors to the Maleny–Montville–Mapleton area have the choice of starting a driving tour from **Landsborough** and finishing at **Nambour**, or the reverse. A longer circuit via the winding roads of Conondale and Kenilworth can be made from Maleny or Mapleton. A visit to Maleny should include the lookouts on Mountain View Road along the southern escarpment – the best spots are **McCarthys Lookout** and **Mary Cairncross Park**. The **Baroon Pocket Dam** on Obi Obi Creek, a known platypus habitat flowing through the north of the town, is accessed through Maleny.

Mary Cairncross Scenic Reserve

A 65 ha patch of untouched rainforest is preserved on the southern escarpment of the Blackall Range near Maleny.

The Mary Cairncross Scenic Reserve is recognised as one of the best examples of Australia's remnant subtropical rainforest. A diorama depicting the rainforest through time is at the entrance to a 2-km walk on which visitors can experience the rainforest environment and its plants such as red cedars, black apple trees and strangler figs (*right*), wildlife such as the Red-necked Wallaby (*left*), brush-turkeys, whipbirds and Wompoo Fruit-Doves. The picnic area has scenic views.

Montville

A quaint place on a mountain ridge, Montville has the feel of an English village. It even has a village green, a village hall, tiny wooden churches, and a timber restaurant that was the original general store. Garden paths meander through a maze of shops, potteries and galleries.

Eclectic architecture includes Tudor, Irish and English cottages built in log and stone, Swiss and Bavarian chalets, colonial Queenslanders and an old mill water-wheel. Accommodation within the village and immediate surrounds includes motel suites, guest houses, bed and breakfasts and private cabins.

A heritage trail is signposted throughout the village and a **Senses Trail** for the visually impaired, created by the Country Women's Association, starts near the village hall and crosses a pedestrian bridge to **Razorback Lookout**, with panoramic views to the coast.

A walking track to **Lake Baroon** begins at Montville and walks to the north-west lead to **Kondalilla National Park** with its spectacular waterfalls and rainforest.

Lake Baroon The Baroon Pocket Dam on Obi Obi Creek between Maleny and Mapleton is great for picnics and boating.

Above: **Montville** Midway along the Blackall Range, Montville's Main Street is a string of galleries, art and craft shops, cottages and cafés.

Flaxton and Mapleton

Before the road along the Blackall Range descends to Nambour you pass through two more villages in the style of Montville, only smaller – Flaxton and Mapleton.

Flaxton, overlooking Nambour, has a vineyard, a museum and a **miniature English Village** (Flaxton Dr, 9.30 a.m. – 5 p.m. Ph: 07 5445 7225).

Mapleton is the gateway to the **Mapleton Falls National Park** and the lush **Mapleton State Forest**. In the centre of the hamlet, on Delicia Road, is **Lilyponds Park**, a popular picnic spot with a children's playground and a pond frequented by waterbirds.

Riding the Range

The picturesque towns of Maleny, Montville, Flaxton and Mapleton sit on the spine of the Blackall Range. Once covered by rainforest and eucalypt forest, the range today is a mix of remnant and regrowth forest, planted trees and gardens and open grassy ridges.

The road follows the range top and has views to the coast and the ranges to the west.

Kenilworth and Conondale

The road west from Maleny takes you to Conondale and Kenilworth in the upper Mary River Valley. Here you traverse isolated, rugged country with steep, forest-covered ranges falling to rich river valleys. It is splendidly scenic terrain.

Conondale is the town nearest the source of the Mary River, high in the Conondale Range. Five kilometres west of the town is an access road to **Conondale National Park**, which protects a large part of the range. A drive from Conondale to Kenilworth passes through part of the **Imbil State Forest**, one of the largest State forests in the region.

Kenilworth is a historic dairying and timbergetting town at the junction of the Obi Obi Creek with the Mary River. The town's dairying heritage is continued at the **Kenilworth Country Foods Cheese Factory** (Cnr Elizabeth & Charles Sts, Kenilworth, Ph: 07 5446 0144). The factory makes specialty cheese and yoghurt and has a tasting room where you can sample the products and a viewing area to watch cheesemaking.

Just outside of the town is the historic **Kenilworth Homestead**, where you can enjoy grass and water slides, pony rides and canoeing and fishing on the Mary River (2760 Eumundi-Kenilworth Rd, Ph: 07 5446 0555 – bookings required).

Above: **Flaxton Gardens; Mapleton Tavern** Flaxton and Mapleton are both interesting towns towards the northern end of the Blackall Range crest.

Sunshine Coast Great Walk

One of six Great Walks being developed by the Queensland Parks and Wildlife Service, the Sunshine Coast Great Walk is expected to take hikers on a journey through the wild and spectacular parts of the **Blackall Range**. This is a high, rugged region of great natural beauty, yet it is only 30 km in a straight line from the coast and is close to the towns of **Maleny** and **Montville**, which sit on top of the range. The walk traverses scenic areas including **Kondalilla National Park**, **Maleny Forest Reserve**, **Delicia Road Conservation Park** and **Mapleton Forest Reserve**. Walks range from short day hikes to treks of up to four days with overnight stops. Most of the walks in the total 45 km of tracks are classed as easy, but some are more challenging, catering for the more experienced bushwalker. Highlights include the tumbling, 80-m **Kondalilla Falls** and waterhole, **Mapleton Falls Lookout**, **Obi Obi Gorge** and **Obi Obi Creek**, **Cherrulla Creek and Falls**, **Baxter Creek** and the **Baxter Valley**. Walkers will have expansive views across the ranges and pass through heathland, wet and dry sclerophyll forest, notophyll vine forest, tall eucalypt forest and subtropical rainforest, each with a wide variety of wildlife. Walks can be started from a number of set-off points at both ends of the trail and in the mid-section.

Baroon Pocket to Kondalilla National Park

This 10-km Great Walk section starts from **Baroon Pocket Dam** (access via Montville) and heads north to **Kondalilla National Park**, passing through a piccabeen palm gully and forest with large turpentine, blackbutt and brush box trees. The track enters Kondalilla National Park at **Obi Obi Creek** and follows the **Picnic Creek circuit**. Two viewing platforms give you glimpses of the beautiful **Obi Obi Gorge**, the ranges to the west and **Lake Baroon**. The track then winds north below the **Kondalilla Falls**.

Kondalilla Falls One of the spectacles of the Kondalilla National Park. These falls on Skene Creek are accessed from the Picnic Creek picnic area. Kondalilla is an Aboriginal word meaning "rushing waters".

Kondalilla National Park Coastal and inland Aboriginal communities gathered here to harvest and eat the bunya nut. The nut from the bunya pine was an important totem and was associated with spiritual powers and legends.

Maleny Forest Reserve

The Great Walk heads north for about 10 km from **Kondalilla**, across **Flaxton Mill Road** and into the Maleny Forest Reserve, where it follows a forestry road through wet and dry sclerophyll forest before dropping down to **Baxter Creek**, a beautiful rock-strewn creek with dense vine forest. The track then climbs up **Suses Pocket Road Reserve** through lush, tall forest to **Obi Obi Creek Road**, where it follows a footpath and road verge to **Mapleton Falls National Park**.

Left to right: **Mapleton Falls Lookout; Obi Obi Valley from Mapleton Falls Lookout** The Sunshine Coast Great Walk includes the walking circuit through Mapleton Falls National Park with lookouts giving views of the Obi Obi Valley and the Conondale Range to the west.

Wildlife in the Ranges

Clockwise from right: Squirrel Glider; Platypus; Echidna – just three of the wildlife species that live in the hills, valleys and streams of the Blackall Range.

In the **Blackall Range** and the nearby **Conondale Range** just to the west, 107 species of birds, 39 species of mammals, 72 species of reptiles and 32 species of frogs have been recorded. Three of the frogs – the Southern Day Frog, the Pouched Frog and the Gastric Brooding Frog – are threatened species. The Gastric Brooding Frog, discovered at Picnic Creek in **Kondalilla National Park** in 1972, has not been seen since 1979. In this unusual frog, tadpoles develop in the female's stomach. The tadpoles produce a substance that prevents the female from secreting her gastric juices until they are released out of her mouth as live young.

The waterways of the area are extremely important habitats for Platypus, particularly **Obi Obi Creek**, which rises near Maleny and flows down the western side of the Blackall Range and into the Mary River. The streams, also home to freshwater crayfish, are protected where they flow through national parks and conservation reserves, but many of them start in private property along the crest of the range, increasing the risk of pollution that can affect wildlife and vegetation downstream.

Mapleton Falls

When the Great Walk enters **Mapleton Falls National Park** it passes near Mapleton Falls and around the **Wompoo Circuit** to exit in the north-east corner of the park. Mapleton Falls National Park has one of the most spectacular lookouts on the **Blackall Range** – cliff tops, cut by waterfalls, provide views over piccabeen forest to the **Conondale Range**.

Delicia Road Conservation Park to Mapleton Forest Reserve

From **Mapleton Falls National Park** the track follows a road to **Delicia Road Conservation Park** and into the southern side of the large **Mapleton Forest Reserve**, where it makes a great 25 km loop to the north-west to **Cheerulla camping area** (the walk's northernmost point) and back. Part of the track follows a ridge high above the eastern side of **Cheerulla Valley** and then along **Cheerulla Creek**. As well as the Cheerulla camping area there are two other campsites on the loop. The Mapleton Forest Reserve track has some steep sections and is for the experienced and well-prepared walker. Vegetation to be seen includes tallowwood and brush box, grass-trees, heath and stands of casuarinas. Rock orchids and ferns can be found on many of the sheltered rock outcrops.

Mapleton Forest Reserve Covering the north-western section of the Blackall Range, this large area of State forest stretches from Mapleton almost to Kenilworth. More than 25 km of the 45 km Sunshine Coast Hinterland Great Walk runs over the forest's ridges and valleys through spectacular scenery that includes eucalypt forests and rainforest swith gorges, running creeks and waterfalls.

The Eastern Rosella *(right)* is one of more than 100 species of birds in the Blackall Range region. They also include the Peregrine Falcon, often seen soaring above Mapleton Falls, and the Wompoo Fruit-Dove, whose booming call can be heard for up to 1 km as it feeds among the tree-tops.

Top to botttom: **Nambour nestled at the foot of the Blackall Ranges; Rural mural.**

Top to bottom: **Fairhill Gardens at Yandina; The popular Eumundi Markets.**

North Along the Inland Route

The **Bruce Highway**, the main route from Brisbane to north Queensland, is a 110-km/h four-lane highway through the Sunshine Coast region, reverting to two lanes just past Yandina. Much of it has been constructed in recent times on new alignments, leaving the **old Bruce Highway** that passed through towns like **Caboolture**, **Beerwah**, **Nambour**, **Yandina** and **Eumundi** free of through-traffic and making the old highway and the myriad roads that meander off it through the countryside ideal for daytrippers. The coastal region from Caloundra to Noosa follows the north-south artery of the **Nicklin Way** and the **Sunshine Motorway** for easy travel from the hinterland to your beach of choice.

Palmview to Nambour

On the Bruce Highway at **Palmview**, just past the Caloundra exit, is **Aussie World**, a fairground park with rides, games and the **Ettamogah Pub** (Frizzo Rd, Bruce Highway, Palmview, Ph: 07 5494 5444). Further north is the **Forest Glen Deer Sanctuary** (Tanawha Tourist Drive, Forest Glen, Ph: 07 5445 1274).

The next major exit is the **Nambour Connection Road** and **Maroochydore Road**. On the road to **Nambour** is the Sunshine Coast's first major theme park – **The Big Pineapple**, built in 1971.

Diversions from Nambour lead to the quiet towns of **Palmwoods** and **Woombye**. Nambour, originally a sugar mill town, is the gateway to the range-top towns of **Mapleton**, **Montville** and **Maleny**. A round trip from Nambour through these towns circuits back via **Landsborough** to the Bruce Highway.

Forest Glen Deer Sanctuary Visitors can drive through the 60-acre safari, feed deer, cuddle a Koala or watch the daily park ranger show.

Ettamogah Pub Aussie World's Australiana pub is based on a pub from a popular cartoon.

Yandina to Eumundi

North of Nambour, on the old Bruce Highway, is Yandina – the Sunshine Coast's oldest town, established in 1871. **Yandina Historical House** is a museum of early times. More of a tourist drawcard is Yandina's **Ginger Factory** (Pioneer Rd, Yandina, Ph: 07 5446 7100). Nearby is the **Nutworks Macadamia Nut Factory**. Yandina also has a **country music Hall of Fame** and the **Fairhill Botanical Gardens**, which specialise in native plants. Picnic spots in the area include **Wappa and Cooloolabin Dams** and **Point Glorious Lookout**.

Eumundi, north of Yandina and inland from Noosa, is another historic town of the region. Since

Indigenous dancers at the Eumundi Markets teach visitors about Aboriginal culture.

being bypassed by the Bruce Highway it has become a popular place with daytrippers who wander the main street among restored old buildings and shady trees planted to memorialise soldiers. The **Eumundi Markets** are the best markets on the Sunshine Coast and every Wednesday and Saturday the main street and adjacent park are transformed into a colourful and crowded marketplace with over 200 stalls selling a range of wares from handicrafts to furniture, pottery, clothing, fruit and vegetables.

Fruit-themed Fun

Three of the most popular attractions on the Sunshine Coast are based on farm produce – pineapples, ginger and macadamia nuts.

Pineapples, one of the area's long-time crops are the focus at **The Big Pineapple** (*top right*) near **Nambour** (Nambour Connection Road, Woombye, Ph: 07 5442 1333). The theme park displays a variety of tropical fruits and has a rainforest walk and wildlife garden. Entry is free but there are fees for rides. A café and restaurant on site specialise in dishes using fresh tropical fruits.

The **Ginger Factory** (50 Pioneer Rd, Yandina, Ph: 07 5446 7100), originally built at Buderim, was re-built at Yandina and made into a theme park. It offers tours telling the story of ginger from farm to food products and the root's use in cooking and health. The Ginger Train (*bottom right*) runs through tropical gardens. The Ginger Shop sells a range of ginger products. Entry is free.

Nutworks Macadamia Nut Factory (37 Pioneer Rd, Yandina, Ph: 07 5472 7777) welcomes visitors from 9 a.m. – 5 p.m. daily and features the indigenous macadamia nut.

Cooroy and Pomona

These two pretty towns off the highway in the Noosa hinterland were established in the late 19th century as rural centres. Cooroy and Pomona, like Nambour and Yandina, are both on the main northern rail line. **Cooroy**, with pleasant streetscaping and renovated buildings, has cafés, restaurants, gift shops and galleries along its main street, and an old butter factory has been transformed into a theatre.

Pomona, nestled under the towering **Mount Cooroora**, comes to life each July with the **King of the Mountain Festival**, when runners from all over the world race up the 439-m mountain. The town also has the **Noosa Shire Museum** (29 Factory St, Pomona, Ph: 07 5485 1080), a railway station that has been turned into a gallery, and the historic **Majestic Theatre** (3 Factory St, Pomona, Ph: 07 5485 2330), established in 1921, which screens movies from the silent era with live organ accompaniment.

Gympie

Famous as the town that saved Queensland from bankruptcy after gold was found there in 1867, Gympie's mining heritage is preserved in many of the town's historic buildings and at the impressive **Historical and Gold Mining Museum** (215 Brisbane Rd, Gympie, Ph: 07 5482 3995). Visitors can pan for gold at the **Deep Creek Fossicking Area**. The history of the forestry industry is on display at the **WoodWorks Forestry and Timber Museum** (Cnr Bruce Hwy & Fraser Rd, Gympie, Ph: 07 5483 7691).

Above, left and right: **Gympie Gold Mining Museum** has a wonderful collection of mining equipment, much of it in working order. Outbuildings and authentic huts display all aspects of the life and daily tasks of the miners who worked with pick and shovel deep underground in shafts below where the city now stands. Gympie is also the base for the Mary Valley Heritage Railway which runs the "Mary Valley Rattler" historic steam train on an 80-km trip through forests and hamlets.

Off and Racing

The annual **Burrandowan Picnic Races** (Burrandowan, Ph: 07 4164 8147) are one of the premier social events of the South Burnett.

The race meeting is held each May at Burrandowan, a cattle station about 80 km west of Kingaroy.

It is a full day of bush racing followed by a barbecue and dancing under the stars in true country style.

Booloumba Creek, Conondale National Park, where rainforest surrounds cool, flowing streams.

Bjelke-Petersen Dam and Lake Barambah A water resource and a place for recreation.

West to the Great Dividing Range

South-East Queensland's north-west quarter is graced with lofty mountains and wide, meandering rivers. Over many years these mountains, the remnants of volcanoes from millions of years ago, have been weathered, eroded and shaped into craggy ranges and valleys. Through these valleys wind two major rivers that are the life-blood of the land – the Burnett and the Mary. The **Burnett River** rises near Monto in Central Queensland and flows southward past **Mundubbera** and **Gayndah** before turning north-east to the coast at Bundaberg. It is fed by the rivers and creeks of the **South Burnett**, the rich farming country around **Kingaroy**, **Nanango** and the **Bunya Mountains** on the Great Dividing Range. The **Mary River** flows from the **Conondale Range**, west of **Maleny**, then north through **Gympie** and **Maryborough**.

Towns of the South Burnett

Once frontier cattle country, the South Burnett is now an intensively developed cane and farming region. Daytrippers to the area discover large and small towns that give a snapshot of typical rural Australia.

The principal town is **Kingaroy**, long known as Australia's peanut capital and home to the **Peanut Heritage Museum** (Haly St, Kingaroy, Ph: 07 4162 4953). It is a typical country town – existing for its rural industries and dependent on them. **Nanango** to Kingaroy's east is a pretty town in the western foothills of the **Brisbane Range**.

From Nanango the visitor can make a 150 km circle tour of the South Burnett through Kingaroy, **Wondai**, **Murgon** and back to Nanango. This trip passes through ever-changing farm and forest country and many small hamlets.

Forests

The South Burnett farmland was once heavily forested and remnants of the native eucalypt forests still cover much of the hills and ridges, creating landscapes that are a mix of clear cultivation and the dark green of untouched scrub. For true, largely untouched wilderness, the **Bunya Mountains**, south-west of Kingaroy, contain extensive rainforest with great stands of massive bunya pines that have been preserved in a national park.

Top to bottom: **Kingaroy; Nanango; Blackbutt; Pioneer Hotel, Linville** Kingaroy is the major town of the region, but Nanango, Blackbutt and Yarraman on the D'Aguilar Highway from Brisbane are passed on the approach to the South Burnett region. Stop off at the Pioneer Hotel at Linville, a historic watering hole that was first built in 1892 at Kannangur and moved to Linville in two parts.

Peanuts and Wine

Each September Kingaroy stages its **Peanut Festival**, a week of entertainment and activities celebrating the peanut, which has given the town prosperity for more than 80 years. Although peanuts are still a major industry in the South Burnett, the rich red volcanic soils and the climate have also proved ideal for wine grapes.

The area has more than 18 wineries and the number is growing. A wine trail to many of the vineyards has been established and a trip through the region is enhanced by sampling the local product. In town, **Kingaroy Wines** (67 William St, Ph: 07 4162 3711) offers tours and tastings of its Stuart Range Estate label.

Bunya Mountains

With their highest point 1135 m above sea level, the Bunya Mountains rise 500 m above the surrounding countryside of the northern Darling Downs and the South Burnett.

From a distance they stand out as a great dark shelf of mountainous country looming over the lighter downs. Up close, the cliffs and steep slopes rear up to the clouds, their peaks covered with rainforest canopy punctured by the protruding upper branches of the towering and majestic bunya pines.

The Bunya Mountains, called *Booburrgan Ngmmun* by the local Aborigines, were a place where clans from South-East Queensland and northern New South Wales gathered for corroborees to feast on the rich bunya nuts.

Bunya Forest Walks Walking tracks meander through the rainforest in the Bunya Mountains National Park.

Bountiful Bunya Pine

The world's largest stand of distinctive bunya pines, *Araucaria bidwillii*, is preserved in the **Bunya Mountains National Park**, where their conical tops tower over the rainforest.

Their pineapple-shaped cones weigh up to 10 kg and fall from December to March. Walkers are warned not to linger below the trees at this time.

These majestic trees were once present in large numbers throughout the forests of South-East Queensland, but today they exist only in remnant rainforest. The **Brisbane City Botanic Gardens** has some fine examples of the bunya pine.

Bunya Wildlife

Tame Red-necked Wallabies (*left*) feed at the Dandabah campsite, providing just a glimpse of the wildlife of the Bunya Mountains. In the less-visited forests and streams abounds a diversity of wildlife that includes the Great Barred Frog and the Bunya Mountains Ringtail Possum, which is endemic to the mountains.

Birdlife, too, is prolific and includes brilliantly coloured Australian King Parrots and Crimson Rosellas as well as Satin Bowerbirds and Green Catbirds.

Brush-turkeys are also common and their large nesting mounds are easily spotted.

Walking the Bunyas

The Bunya Mountains are accessible through **Kingaroy** from the north or **Jondaryan** and **Dalby** from the south. **Bunya Mountains Road** follows the mountain crest through the middle of the national park, past woodland, pines and thick forest.

There is a major camp ground at **Dandabah**, near **Mount Mowbullan** (1101 m) at the southern end of the high country, where a broad grassy camping area is almost surrounded by bunya pines and rainforest. Two other smaller camping areas are at **Westcott**, about midway along the crest, and **Burton's Well** near **Mount Kiangarow** (1135 m) at the northern end.

Walking tracks lead you past 35 km of misty rainforest, tangled vine scrubs, eucalypt forest and open grassland. From Dandabah, circuit tracks cut back through stands of giant bunya pines in thick rainforest before passing waterfalls and open grass ridges, called "balds", which give excellent views to the north-east. A series of tracks along Bunya Mountains Road follow the cliffs of the south-western side, looking out over the sweeping plains of the **Darling Downs**.

Above, top to bottom: **Bunya Mountains National Park** Eucalypt scrub and grass-trees give way to grassy balds and bunya pines.

Cooloola Coast

As the volcanic highlands of eastern Australian slowly eroded, their sands were washed to sea and carried northward by currents or trapped behind rocky outcrops. Wind shaped the multitudinous silicon particles into dunes and plants took hold before being buried under more sand. Being resilient, more plants grew in the humus of the first plants – a process repeated until the great forest-covered sandmasses of **Cooloola** and **Fraser Island** were formed.

Great Sandy National Park

Today Cooloola, from **Noosa** to **Rainbow Beach** and up to the World-Heritage-listed Fraser Island, which stretches another 120 km northward, are protected as the Great Sandy National Park.

Top to bottom: **Four-wheel-driving on Cooloola Beach; Cooloola National Park; Teewah Coloured Sands** Cooloola has vista after scenic vista – long beaches, wildflowers in the heaths, paperbark swamps and coloured sand cliffs.

Abundant Birdlife

Great Sandy National Park is home to over 300 species of birds ranging from Emus to kingfishers, such as the Forest Kingfisher (*right*).

The Emus are one of the few remaining populations in coastal Queensland. The park is also one of the most northerly habitats of the rare Ground Parrot, a shy and elusive green bird mottled with yellow and black, which can be seen fluttering low over heath at twilight.

Cooloola, the largest coastal vegetation remnant on the southern Queensland mainland, is home to many species of plants and animals whose habitats have been reduced by coastal development. It is a spectacular region of high sand dunes, sand blows, coloured sand cliffs, long beaches, tall forests, freshwater lakes, paperbark swamps and wildflower heaths where ground orchids and Christmas Bells flower in a burst of colour during the spring and summer months.

***Cherry Venture* wreck** The hulk of this small freighter, which was unsalvagable after being driven ashore in 1973, lies rusting on Cooloola Beach 2 km south of Double Island Point.

Exploring Cooloola

Cooloola can be approached through **Pomona** and the unsealed **Cooloola Way**, or through **Gympie** and **Tin Can Bay Road**. Sand tracks suitable only for four-wheel-drive lead to camping grounds at **Harrys**, **Fig Tree Point** and **Freshwater**. The Freshwater Road exits to the beach and campsites along **Teewah Beach**. Permits are required.

Walking tracks, including the **Cooloola Wilderness Trail**, lead from these campsites though forest and heathland to the upper reaches of the **Noosa River** and to many perched freshwater lakes and swamps high in the dunes. At the east and north, the Cooloola sandmass meets the Pacific Ocean in a line of spectacular coloured sand cliffs and beautiful beaches, with the rocky headland of **Double Island Point** jutting out, joined by a narrow neck of delicate dunes.

A tree-lined lake at Kinaba Tranquil places await those who venture into the upper parts of the Noosa River.

Bottlenose Dolphins, and rarer Indo-Pacific Humpback Dolphins, visit Tin Can Bay.

Rainbow Beach

Cooloola's beaches and coloured cliffs run from the mouth of the **Noosa River** to **Double Island Point** and around the spectacular Rainbow Beach to Rainbow Beach township and **Inskip Point**, the gateway to the southern end of **Fraser Island**.

Decayed plant matter leaching through the sandmass over thousands of years has coloured it in hues of red, yellow and brown. And where the high dunes and ocean meet, great cliffs of these coloured sands have been sculpted by the eroding forces of the ocean waves. These cliffs are fragile and should be admired from the beach but not climbed.

Four-wheel-drive travel is possible on Cooloola's beaches at low tide. Access is via **Tewantin** at the south, along the **Freshwater Track** just south of Double Island Point, or through Rainbow Beach township. Inexperienced beach drivers should seek local advice as the beaches can be treacherous for vehicles, particularly along Rainbow Beach where the waves break against the cliffs and there are no exits.

Kinaba Information Centre on the upper Noosa River is accessible only by canoe.

Lake Country

The Noosa River rises in the high forested dunes of the Cooloola sandmass and makes its way through everglade swamps and broad shallow lakes to the sea at Noosa Head.

These lakes – Cooroibah and Cootharaba are the largest – are popular for boating and sailing and the starting point for canoeing adventures up the river through the swamps. In places, the winding channels through the paperbarks are barely wide enough to paddle.

Cooloola Beach stretches from the Noosa River mouth (*foreground*) to Double Island Point

Tin Can Bay

The Cooloola sandmass ends at Tin Can Bay Inlet, at the southern end of the **Great Sandy Strait** between **Fraser Island** and the mainland. With a narrow entrance from the ocean between **Inskip Point** and **Hook Point** on Fraser Island, the inlet forms a waterway into the north-west corner of Cooloola and is a popular boating and fishing spot accessed from the sleepy seaside town of Tin Can Bay.

Dolphins visit Tin Can Bay and are commonly seen off the fishing villages and campsites of **Tinnanbar**, **Poona** and **Boonooroo**.

Rainbow Beach, near Double Island Point Sand dunes dominate the low isthmus.

Cook's Comments

"The land hereabouts, which is of moderate height, appears more barren than any we have yet seen upon this coast, the soil more sandy." This is how Captain James Cook described Fraser Island in 1770.

He was right about the sand – the island is almost entirely sand! But, were he able to see the perched lakes, massive forests and streams, he may have been more complimentary.

Top to bottom: The ocean beach north of Indian Head; Beach fishing; Playing on a sand dune; A log bridge over a rainforest creek.

Fraser Island

Vast rainforests crown sand dunes hundreds of metres deep, freshwater lakes perch in the scrub-covered terrain, crystal-clear springs cascade onto broad beaches where cliffs of coloured sands rise like cathedral spires out of the windswept mist – visitors to Fraser Island can expect to witness firsthand the artistry of nature. But Fraser Island is not only the earth's largest sand island, it is a complex ecosystem for plants, mammals, birds, reptiles, fish, insects and microbes – by any measure one of the great natural wonders of the world.

Geography

Fraser Island forms the eastern boundary of **Hervey Bay** and stands just off the Queensland coast, keeping a northward compass as the mainland turns north-westward.

The island is over 120 km long and up to 30 km wide and the forested high dunes reach 250 m above sea level. The Pacific Ocean pounds its eastern beaches for more than 100 km from **Hook Point** to **Indian Head**, and on to **Sandy Cape**, where the dunes flatten and run out to the bare **Breaksea Spit**. Down the western side are sheltered mangroves and inlets. Towards the southern end is low scrubby heath and grassland vivid with wildflowers in spring and summer. Fraser Island's spine is made up of high dunes and deep valleys hidden by forests and dense undergrowth – all thriving on sand.

Great blows of pure white sand stand out against a cloudless sky on Fraser Island.

Streams of fresh, clear water flow through many of Fraser Island's dune forests.

Exploring Fraser Island

Fraser Island is almost entirely national park, part of the **Great Sandy National Park**, which also covers **Cooloola** on the mainland.

The island can be explored by vehicle (four-wheel-drive only) or by hiking. Vehicle tracks crisscross much of the island and generally taper off to dozens of walking tracks. A large part of the island's central region is also included in the **Fraser Island Great Walk**.

Camping grounds on the island's ocean side include **Waddy Point**, **Dundubara** and some sections of the southern beach, where signed. On the western side, camp grounds are at **Wathumba**, **Ungowa** and **Garry's Anchorage**. Inland you can camp at **Lake McKenzie** (hikers only), **Lake Benaroon** (hikers only), **Central Station** and **Lake Boomanjin**. Queensland Parks and Wildlife Service vehicle and camping permits are required (Ph: 131304).

Privately operated campsites and accommodation are located at **Cathedral Beach**, **Eurong** and **Dilli Village**. For those seeking a more luxurious holiday on Fraser Island, resorts operate at **Kingfisher Bay** on the western side and at **Happy Valley** on the eastern side.

Eliza Fraser

Originally called *K'gari*, meaning paradise, by the native Butchulla people, the name Fraser Island followed the shipwreck of the *Stirling Castle* off the coast in 1836. Survivors reached Fraser Island by longboat, where they met a hostile reception from the Aborigines who speared the captain, James Fraser, and captured his wife, Eliza. In the nine weeks that followed, while other survivors reached safety and a rescue party returned, Eliza Fraser was treated harshly by her captors.

A Wealth of Wildlife

The diverse wildlife on Fraser Island makes it of great interest to scientists and conservationists. For those who simply enjoy sharing this beautiful environment with its natural inhabitants, it is a place of wonder.

Among the more than 300 species of birds on the island are the Osprey (*below left*) and the Pacific Baza (*right*). Others include Australia's stork, the Jabiru, the White-bellied Sea-Eagle, cockatoos, lorikeets, parrots, pigeons and kingfishers. On the beach you can see many varieties of seabirds, including the Pied Oystercatcher, searching the sand for eugaries. Fraser Island, like many of the wetlands along the southern Queensland coast, is an important stopover habitat for migratory birds and surrounding swamps are home to wading birds and ducks of many kinds.

Several species of reptiles live among the swamps and forests, including venomous snakes such as the Taipan and the Common Death Adder (*below right*). Amphibians, such as the Ornate Burrowing Frog (*below centre*) are also found. A highlight is to watch freshwater turtles in Lake Alom, a small perched lake in the north of the island, but visitors are asked not to feed them.

Mammals are also represented with wallabies, possums, flying foxes and Dingos inhabiting the island. The Dingos are believed to be some of the purest of the species as they are isolated from domestic dogs. Echidnas are also found on Fraser. The island's surrounding waters are a sanctuary for Dugong, dolphins, and Loggerhead Turtles, which struggle across the beach near Sandy Cape, at the north-west of the island, to lay their eggs. When the eggs hatch, the tiny hatchlings run the gauntlet, avoiding the searching eyes of crows, gulls, hawks and other predators to reach the water.

From August to November, majestic Humpback Whales pass by the eastern side of the island, delighting whale watchers.

Flora and Forests

Seen from the air, Fraser Island is an expanse of deep olive and emerald, broken only by the stark white of sand blows and the mirror-like lakes that dot the high country. An incredible variety of more than 600 plant species grow in the rainforests, paperbark swamps, heaths and on the foreshores.

Most spectacular are the large trees that grow in the high dunes of the island's centre. Here, they thrive on their own decayed, fallen leaves and the humus of companion plants that have been broken down by insects and organisms, turning sterile sand into a smorgasbord of plant food. These great trees – hoop, slash and kauri pines, turpentines, backbutt, tallowwood, brush box and beech – cover a third of a million hectares in a 60 km strip down the island's spine. One of the majestic turpentines is the giant rough-barked satinay, found only on Fraser Island and Cooloola. They grow to more than 50 m high with girths of up to 18 m. In 1925, large numbers of these trees were felled and shipped away to be used as piles in the walls of the Suez Canal, as well as in the construction of many Australian wharves.

Tropical vegetation is prolific in the island's forests – palms, ferns, elkhorns, staghorns, crows nests, orchids – and, in the understorey, fungi grow on decaying logs.

Cycads, seen here in open scrub near a sand blow, are found in many places on Fraser Island.

Pandanus These small, spreading trees, resistant to salt and spray, cling precariously to sand cliffs above the beaches.

Fraser Island Great Walk

One of a number of specially planned walks in major Queensland national parks, the Fraser Island Great Walk passes through some of the island's special places in the forests that shroud the high dunes. It includes **Lake McKenzie, Central Station, Wanggoolba Creek, Lake Wabby** and the **Valley of the Giants**. Walkers can take short walks, day walks, or treks of up to three days. The track starts at **Dilli Village**, once a sand-mining company camp, and finishes at **Happy Valley**.

Rainforest tranquillity Fern-lined creeks abound in the forests of the island and their cool cocoon of greenery can be enjoyed on many walks, including sections of the Fraser Island Great Walk.

Here you'll experience an amazing variety of landscapes, including ocean and estuarine beaches, cliffs of coloured sand, gorges, dense rainforest, tall open forest and the world's largest perched lake, **Lake Boomanjin**.

Dilli Village to Central Station

The first section is a 6.3 km track to **Lake Boomanjin**. The walk then skirts around the lake and on to **Lake Benaroon** (7.2 km).

The next section to Central Station, 7.5 km, passes **Lake Birabeen** and **Lake Jennings** and into massive brush box and satinay forest. You descend into historic Central Station, once the island's forestry headquarters, set among vine forest, kauri pine and palms on Wanggoolba Creek.

Campsites are at Lake Boomanjin, Lake Benaroon and Central Station.

Central Station to Lake Wabby

From Central Station walkers have the option of two routes to **Lake McKenzie** and **Lake Wabby**. One is a 6.6 km trip via **Basin Lake** to the white sandy shores of Lake McKenzie, then 16.2 km on to Lake Wabby.

Sand tracks among the tall timbers All vehicle tracks on Fraser Island require four-wheel-drives. Some are easy, like the one shown above, some are difficult and require careful driving and experience. Novice drivers should seek advice.

The second (11.3 km) is to take the Wanggoolba Creek boardwalk and the first 2 km of the Pile Valley circuit and along an old logging tram line route to Lake McKenzie before travelling to Lake Wabby.

Both options provide an excellent two-day walk between Central Station and Lake McKenzie. Walkers who want to cover both tracks can return to Central Station from Lake McKenzie and take the option two route to Lake Wabby with a diversion to Lake McKenzie if desired. Lake McKenzie has a campsite. Lake Wabby does not have a camp ground but walkers can exit to the beach.

The Parks and Wildlife Service has also developed a number of connecting tracks in the popular Central Station, Lake McKenzie and **Eurong** areas. One of these is a walking track between **Kingfisher Bay** on the west coast and Central Station, then on to Eurong on the east coast.

Lake Wabby This beautiful freshwater lake just north of Eurong is behind a sand blow close to the ocean beach and can be reached along a walking track from the beach. Sand blown in on the ocean winds is continually encroaching on the lake

Indian Head This massive headland, named because its profile resembles an American Indian's face, dominates the island's ocean beach. A walk to its top gives spectacular views of the island and beaches and is a perfect place to watch passing whales.

Dingos

Fraser Island's Dingos, which can often be seen prowling the beaches (*right*) or hanging around campsites, are a genetically pure strain of Australia's native dog.

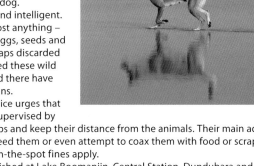

They are wild, unpredictable, cunning and intelligent. Though naturally lean, Dingos will eat almost anything – wallabies and other native animals, turtle eggs, seeds and berries if necessary, and certainly camp scraps discarded thoughtlessly by humans. When people feed these wild creatures they can become threatening and there have been tragic incidents of contact with humans.

The Queensland Parks and Wildlife Service urges that children and teenagers should always be supervised by adults and that people should stay in groups and keep their distance from the animals. Their main advice is **never feed Dingos** – it is an offence to feed them or even attempt to coax them with food or scraps. The maximum penalty is $3000 but $225 on-the-spot fines apply.

Fenced campgrounds have been established at Lake Boomanjin, Central Station, Dundubara and Waddy Point to keep Dingos away. An information pack on the animal is supplied with camping permits.

Beach and bush Beach fishing (*top*) is popular on the island. A boardwalk (*bottom*) follows a pretty creek.

Lake Wabby to Valley of the Giants

The Great Walk north from Lake Wabby to the Valley of the Giants is for experienced bushwalkers. It is through remote country and requires a high degree of self-reliance as the distance between campsites is 16.2 km and the track has long, steep slopes and other hazards. From Lake Wabby the route heads north-west, connecting with old forestry roads in the thick forests of the central high dunes.

From here it follows a ridge forested with tall blackbutt and descends into valleys between high dunes blanketed in rainforest. Here, the Valley of the Giants, has some of the largest trees on the island. There is also a campsite where you can relax before your next trek on the Great Walk.

Valley of the Giants to Happy Valley

The 13.1 km section between the Valley of the Giants and **Lake Garawongera** goes through some of the most impressive brush box, satinay forest and rainforest on the island before opening out onto the beautiful Lake Garawongera campsite. The final 6.6 km section of the Fraser Island Great Walk takes you from Lake Garawongera to Happy Valley on the island's east coast.

Lovely Lakes

Fraser Island has some of the world's best examples of the geological phenomenon known as a perched lake.

Usually, sand is not watertight, so how does the water in these beautiful lakes perched high above sea level not leach away through the sandy dunes? The story begins at the time of the island's formation when sand was washed and blown from the beaches to become the island's first dunes. Plants began to grow on the dunes – plants that would be covered by sand, followed by more plants and more sand over thousands of years to make Fraser Island the great sand island it is today. Over thousands of years, decaying vegetation settled into depressions in the high dunes and cemented tiny sand particles together, forming a soft sandstone that would eventually hold water.

As the perched lakes formed in these depressions, around their edges grew paperbarks, reeds and swamp grasses, dropping more plant matter which settled as sediment in the lakes' bottoms, boosting their ability to hold water. Today, the lakes are large bodies of clear, clean, fresh water surrounded by dazzling white beaches.

The biggest of Fraser Island's perched lakes is **Lake Boomanjin**, inland from Dilli Village towards the south of the island. Boomanjin covers an area of almost 200 ha. The highest is **Lake Bowarrady** at 120 m above sea level.

Fraser Island lakes Two of the many picturesque freshwater lakes high in the dunes of Fraser Island.

Maryborough and Hervey Bay

The Queensland coastal region from Maryborough to Bundaberg is known as the **Fraser Coast**, taking its name from the nearby massive sand island across Hervey Bay and the Great Sandy Strait. The coast around the **Mary River** mouth has only a few isolated, tiny settlements. But just north of Maryborough is Hervey Bay, a booming holiday city and whale-watching mecca. North-west is the cane-growing area around the town of **Childers** on the Bruce Highway. The Fraser Coast has a number of significant and varied national parks, including the **Burrum Coast National Park** north and south of the **Burrum River**, **Poona National Park** just south of the Mary River mouth, and, in the mountain country behind Childers, the **Goodnight Scrub and Mount Walsh national parks**.

Maryborough

One of Queensland's oldest cities, Maryborough is a graceful blend of the old world with the new in a pleasant subtropical city. With a historic past as a major colonial immigration port, the city reclining beside the **Mary River** has many striking colonial buildings and scores of "Queenslander" style houses from the 19th and 20th centuries. In the Wharf Street precinct, the colonial **Customs House** and **Bond Store** are museums, and visitors to the region can research immigrant history at the **Heritage Centre**.

Maryborough Post Office One of the many striking colonial-era buildings that give Maryborough its character. Among them is Brennan & Geraghty's corner store, preserved by the National Trust as a time capsule of the days before supermarkets.

Maryborough Town Hall is just a block from the beautiful Queens Park, on the southern bank of the Mary River where it makes a loop around the city centre. Free, guided heritage walks are held each weekday morning.

The colonial era buildings are complemented by wide, tree-lined streets and shady gardens featuring palms and other tropical and subtropical plants. The 100-year-old **Queens Park** adds to the tropical atmosphere with a waterfall, lily pond and band rotunda. Maryborough is the gateway to **Fraser Island** and just south of the city on the Bruce Highway is a **Fraser Island Information Centre** where visitors can arrange permits and book accommodation and tours.

Hervey Bay

Once just a cluster of small seaside villages, Hervey Bay is today a large and growing city on the shores of its namesake. The villages of the past – **Point Vernon**, **Pialba**, **Scarness**, **Torquay** and **Urangan** – are now suburbs of the city. **Fraser Island** to the east shelters Hervey Bay's waters from the south-east winds, making it a safe place for boating and its north-facing beaches safe for swimming.

The string of beachfronts from Point Vernon to Urangan has a continuous landscaped esplanade, allowing a pleasant walk beside the blue waters of the bay with views of Fraser Island to the east. Hervey Bay is famed for the passing Humpback Whales, which visit the warm waters of the bay each winter.

Hervey Bay city with the Urangan Boat Harbour in the foreground and Hervey Bay in the background The harbour is a centre for whale-watching cruises in Hervey Bay and passenger and vehicular ferries run to Fraser Island.

Sailing from Hervey Bay The safe waters of the Great Sandy Strait and Hervey Bay are ideal for sailing, boating and fishing. Just across the strait is Fraser Island, whose northern half creates the bay. The strait divides the southern half of the island from the mainland.

Watching Whales

Each winter, one of the wondrous close encounters between humans and sea-dwelling mammals is played out in Hervey Bay as thousands of people take whale watching cruises to see these magnificent beasts at play.

For as long as they have swum the oceans, Humpback Whales have migrated each winter from cold southern seas to the warm waters of the bay to calve, before returning south with their young.

Through most of the 19th and half of the 20th centuries, interaction between humans and whales along the Australian coast was violent and bloody as whalers drove the species to the brink of extinction.

These days, hunting and killing is replaced by respect for these enormous animals, which are among the largest mammals on earth, and people flock to see them in their natural habitat and to learn about their behaviour.

The whales, up to 15 m in length and weighing as much as 45 t, play in safety in the waters of Hervey Bay. They put on an awesome display, lifting their bodies out of the water before crashing back beneath the waves, slapping their giant tails on the water's surface and rolling over and showing off close to the whale-watching tour boats.

Whale-watching cruises, which are strictly controlled by wildlife protection laws, operate out of **Urangan Boat Harbour**.

Torbanlea, Howard and Childers

Northward from Maryborough along the Bruce Highway are the historic former coal mining townships of **Torbanlea** and **Howard**. Both have houses and commercial buildings from their mining heyday; many of them are in the Queenslander style – on high stumps with verandahs all around. Torbanlea boasts the **Burrum Mining Museum** (Union St, Torbanlea, Ph: 07 4129 4122), housing more than 4000 items of memorabilia.

Childers is a pretty town in the middle of rich farming land, its wide main street lined with trees shading the many historic buildings listed by the National Trust as examples of early Queensland architecture. Sugar cane is one of the main crops, but avocados, grapes and vegetables are also grown in the region's fertile volcanic soil.

Burrum Coast National Park

The coast around the mouth of the **Burrum River** north of Maryborough has some of the State's most spectacular wallum wilderness that blossoms in spring and early summer into a wonderland of spectacular wildflowers.

More than 23,000 ha of this land is protected in the Burrum Coast National Park. The park has three sections – **Woodgate** (6000 ha) and **Kinkuna** (13,900 ha) north of the river, and **Burrum River** section (3200 ha) south of the river. The Woodgate section, which surrounds the beach township of Woodgate, is easily accessible by conventional vehicle, but a four-wheel-drive is necessary to reach Kinkuna. Mangrove-lined river banks, wallum heathland, eucalypt and angophora forests, tea-tree swamps and small pockets of palm forests typify the Woodgate section. One 800 m return boardwalk enters tea-tree swamp behind Woodgate township, while three others lead into swamps, open forest and mangroves. One track even has a hide for viewing waterbirds wading on the nearby shallow lake. The Kinkuna section is undeveloped park that is ideal for birdwatching and bushwalking. Like many of the more isolated beaches in the Hervey Bay region, Kinkuna Beach provides a safe hatchery for Loggerhead Turtles.

Great Sandy Strait

To the east of the town of Maryborough lies a long strip of shallow water and sand banks between the coast and the southern half of Fraser Island known as the Great Sandy Strait.

High tide covers many of the sand banks and mangrove flats, but at low tide the strait becomes a maze of sand islands separated by narrow channels and vast areas of exposed mangrove mud.

The region is popular with anglers and crabbers who boat out into the strait from Urangan, the Mary River and fishing hamlets.

Wildlife of the Fraser Coast Feathertail Gliders *(below)* and the common Carpet Python *(left)* are found in the area's national parks.

West of Brisbane

Looking westward from Brisbane on a clear day, you can see the blue-hazed Great Dividing Range lining the horizon. These rugged mountains mark the boundary between the subtropical coastal hinterland and the grazing lands and sparsely wooded aridlands of Outback Queensland.

Superb Fairy-wren

Of Rugged Mountain Ranges

Sandwiched as they are between cultivated land to either side, the forested ridges and valleys of the **Great Dividing Range** are a refuge for a variety of plants and animals. Tall eucalypt forests cloak the ridges and rainforests shelter in the valleys. Creeks and rivers tumble in sparkling cascades or plummet over cliffs in dramatic waterfalls, throwing up clouds of mist that cool the summer air.

The mountain parks are not only a refuge for wildlife; they provide a welcome escape from the noisy, hustle-bustle of urban life. Here you can enjoy a picnic under the shade of tall eucalypts, take a dip in a clear-water pool, or simply close your eyes and listen to the calming sounds of the forest: the musical burble of a mountain stream, the echoing call of a bellbird or the quiet whisper of the breeze through the trees.

All along the escarpment you can admire the spectacular views from the many lookouts dotted along the range, or go in search for clues of the pioneers. With a diversity of plant and animal life, the mountains are a naturalist's and photographer's delight, and many elusive species provide a challenge for the wildlife spotter.

Beyond the Main Range

Beyond the divide lies the fertile expanse of the **Darling Downs**. It is now intensively farmed, but here you'll discover many reminders of the west's pioneering past, including: abandoned mines, charming country towns with wide streets and ornate old hotels, elegant colonial homesteads and the grand public buildings of **Toowoomba** and **Warwick**.

Further to the south, centred on the town of **Stanthorpe**, is the **Granite Belt**, where the cool upland climate favours orchards and wine production. Here are found national parks with amazing granite scenery, including tall spires and precariously balanced boulders.

The Darling Downs

The Darling Downs were first described by the intrepid explorer and botanist Allan Cunningham in 1827. He had been sent by the NSW Governor (Queensland did not exist as a separate colony until 1859) to determine what lay beyond the imposing range of mountains to the west of Moreton Bay.

Cunningham was suitably impressed by what he found, reporting that the expanse of grassy plains was the finest country he had yet seen in his travels. He went on to name the new discovery in honour of his master, Governor Ralph Darling.

Encouraged by Cunningham's glowing account, settlers soon ventured to the Downs, and Jandowae Pub (*top*) and Maryvale Farm (*bottom*) are reminders of the early days of settlement.

Top to bottom: **Toowoomba City Hall; Carr's Lookout, Scenic Rim; The town hall and Criterion Hotel, Warwick; Girraween National Park.**

Toowoomba

Perched on the edge of the **Great Dividing Range** escarpment is Queensland's largest provincial city and the gateway to the rich agricultural lands of the **Darling Downs**. From its humble beginnings as a squatter's run in 1852, Toowoomba has grown into a major regional centre, boasting many grand buildings and over 1044 ha of public parks and gardens. It is for these beautiful green spaces that Toowoomba is perhaps best known today, rightly earning it the epithet "the Garden City". **Picnic Point Lookout** gives sweeping views over the **Lockyer Valley**, but other highlights include strolling through the splendid greenery of **Queens Park and Botanic Gardens**, admiring the stately grandeur of the city centre's public buildings or reliving the colonial past at the **Cobb & Co Museum**.

History and Heritage

The first European settlement established in the area was at **Drayton** in 1842. Drayton soon grew to become a well-established settlement, but by 1850, drought caused many of its inhabitants to re-settle in an area a few miles to the north-east. Drayton's original pub, the **Royal Bulls Head Inn**, which is now owned by the National Trust, still stands as a reminder of those early pioneering days.

Toowoomba's City Hall was completed in 1900.

Royal Bull's Head Inn, Drayton Once acclaimed as the best wayside inn between the coast and the Darling Downs, this is the second of two buildings to have occupied the Bull's Head site. Built in 1858, the inn is now owned by the National Trust.

Some years later, the enterprising squatter Thomas Alford built a homestead, which he named "Toowoomba". His settlement was for many years known locally as "The Swamp", which many believe to be the meaning of the name Toowoomba, but, despite its nickname, it rapidly expanded to outstrip neighbouring Drayton.

By the mid 1860s Toowoomba was a booming agricultural centre. The arrival of the railway in 1867 assured the town's future. During the late 19th century, many of the city's fine buildings, including the **City Hall**, **Post Office**, **Railway Station** and **Alexandra Building**, were constructed.

Alexandra Building The extravagant facade is typical of many of the buildings completed in Toowoomba during the boom times of the late 19th and early 20th centuries. Toowoomba is home to many historic buildings in numerous architectural styles.

Railway Station Built in 1874 from Murphy's Creek stone, the station retains its Victorian elegance. Dine in style in the historic refreshment room, which has remained virtually unchanged since it opened for passengers 130 years ago.

The Garden City

Situated 700 m above sea level on the edge of the escarpment and with an annual rainfall of 950 mm, Toowoomba's seasonal climate provides ideal conditions for horticulture. Early civic leaders recognised this and it is largely to the wealth and vision of the Victorian era that Toowoomba owes its magnificent array of more than 230 public parks and gardens that characterise the city today.

Spring and summer provide stunning floral displays, while in the cooler months the city's many deciduous trees bring a taste of autumn to Queensland as their leaves turn through rich reds to golden brown.

Carnival of Flowers

In celebration of Toowoomba's gardening culture, the city hosts the nationally-renowned Carnival of Flowers every year in late September.

It features a spectacular Grand Parade with colourful floats, musicians and street performers. The city's parks and gardens are at their springtime best and many private gardens are open to the public too. The Carnival is a floral extravaganza not to be missed in the Darling Downs calendar!

Things to See and Do

1 Visit Queens Park and the Botanic Gardens

2 Take in the sights of the city at Picnic Point

3 Step back in time to stagecoach days at the Cobb & Co. Museum (27 Lindsay St, Ph: 07 4639 1971)

4 Get nostalgic for the silver screen days at the heritage-listed Empire Theatre (56 Neil St, Ph: 07 4698 9900)

5 See a replica slab hut from "Our Selection" that stands on the site where author Arthur Hoey Davis, creator of Dad and Dave and better known as Steele Rudd, once lived (Follow the signs from Ruthven St to Greenmount)

Ju Raku En Japanese Garden
A joint project of the University of Southern Queensland and Toowoomba City Council, Ju Raku En translates as "long life and happiness in a public garden".

Highlights of the Garden City's parks include: **Queens Park and Botanic Gardens**, with its mature trees (many of which date from the 1870s) and meticulously laid-out garden beds and lawns; the tranquillity of the streams and waterfalls in the **Ju Raku En Japanese Garden**; the delightful variety of blooms in the **State Rose Garden** in Newtown Park; **Lake Annand** with its New Zealand influences; and the expansive views and bushland setting of the escarpment parks (see over the page).

Left to right: **Queens Park; Queens Park spring flowering; Garden at Picnic Point** Toowoomba has long been recognised for its superb gardens (both public and private) and springtime is undoubtedly the best time to visit the city with its floral displays that rival any in Australia.

Sunflowers are a common sight on the Downs, with fields full of the upturned, golden blooms.

Mustering on horseback is a tradition still very much alive on the Downs.

Sorghum field Rain clouds gather over a crop growing west of the Divide.

Farm near Dalby Inland South-East Queensland is often dry or drought-stricken.

Toowoomba Surrounds

West from Toowoomba and the **Great Dividing Range** is the great, rolling expanse of the **Darling Downs**, some of the most productive agricultural land in Australia. A wide range of crops – including wheat, barley, oats, sorghum, chickpeas, and cotton – are grown on the gently undulating plains and hills, creating a vivid patchwork of colours and textures across the landscape. Golden fields of sunflowers are especially striking, with their massed faces all upturned to the warm sunshine. Beef cattle, pigs and sheep are the main livestock industries and you may still see jackaroos and jillaroos mustering on horseback in the Darling Downs, as they and their forebears have done for over 150 years.

The region's proud rural heritage is reflected in the many towns and villages of the Downs. They seem little changed from colonial times, with cool, shaded footpaths lining wide main streets and elegant two-storey pubs with decorated ironwork poised strategically on the crossroads. Many of the old homesteads retain their colonial character – some fashioned grandly from stone; others more modest weatherboard affairs.

Jondaryan Woolshed

One of the best places to experience the rich pastoral heritage of the Darling Downs is the **Jondaryan Woolshed** (Evanslea Rd, Jondaryan, 9 a.m.–4 p.m. Ph: 07 4692 2229 for entry fee).

Here you can listen to the story of the Darling Downs' rural pioneers and discover the exciting history of what was once Queensland's largest freehold sheep station. At the time of its completion in 1861, Jondaryan Woolshed was Queensland's biggest and most advanced shearing shed.

Today, you'll find dynamic displays and exhibits and a reconstructed historic village with original equipment in working order. You can watch demonstrations of pastoral skills including blacksmithing and, of course, shearing.

A great time to visit is during the nine-day annual **Australian Heritage Festival** (usually held in late August), when hundreds of volunteers bring the woolshed and village alive.

Jondaryan Woolshed features demonstrations of sheep shearing.

Koala Conservation

One of the greatest threats to wildlife in Australia today is the loss of habitat. Koalas are among the many animals suffering due to a decline in their preferred home environment. In the extensively farmed Darling Downs efforts are now being made to protect Koalas' remaining refuges, especially around **Oakey**.

Once numbering millions in Queensland, Koala populations have been drastically reduced, but they are still managing to hold on in the west in isolated pockets, such as treed roadside verges and in gum trees along watercourses.

Museum of Australian Army Flying, Oakey

Another museum telling an equally interesting, if quite different, story is the **Museum of Australian Army Flying**, located at nearby Oakey (Army Airfield, Oakey, open 10 a.m.–4 p.m. Wed to Sun, Ph: 07 4691 7666). Here you'll find one of the best displays of aviation history in Australia, with examples of every kind of aircraft flown by the Australian Army since World War II, as well as some famous flying machines like the Spitfire, and replicas of Sir Charles Kingsford-Smith's Southern Cross and German WWI Ace Baron von Richthoffen's bright red tri-plane.

Escarpment Parks

From **Toowoomba**, it is only a short trip to the many escarpment parks that fringe the eastern edge of the city. There are seven parks in all, including (from north to south) **Jubilee**, **Redwood**, **Table Top**, **Picnic Point**, **McKnight**, **Duggan** and **Glen Lomond**.

All of the parks offer a range of graded walks from short, easy strolls to longer, steeper trails for the more energetic. Escarpment Bushwalks brochures are available from the **Tourist Information Centre**. Picnic Point is the most popular of the parks, favoured for its stunning views over the **Lockyer Valley** and beyond. The distinctive Table Top, with its naturally treeless summit, eclipses Picnic Point for vistas, but it comes at the cost of a steep 1.9-km return walk.

Picnic Point Lookout One of seven escarpment parks that fringe Toowoomba, Picnic Point is the most easily accessible and offers superb views over the Lockyer Valley.

Crows Nest National Park

Beautiful bushland can also be found a little further afield at **Crows Nest National Park** (approximately 56 km north of **Toowoomba**, camping permitted). Set on the edge of the Great Dividing Range, the park's main feature is **Crows Nest Creek**, which runs in a series of delightful cascades and pools through dry eucalypt country, then dramatically plunges into a granite gorge lined with river she-oaks and forest red gums. A number of well-graded walks give access to the creek and falls.

The park is a must for wildlife-lovers, with shy Brush-tailed Rock-wallabies and Platypus to be found. At night, gliders volplane amongst the eucalypts – the park is home to three species (Sugar, Feathertail and Greater Gliders), as well as Koalas and Common Brushtail Possums. In the spring and summer months the bush resounds to the calls of thornbills, Golden Whistlers, Eastern Spinebills, Grey fantails and Blue-faced Honeyeaters in search of nectar.

Above, left to right: **The pretty Blue-faced Honeyeater** is one of the many nectar-eating birds to be found in Crows Nest National Park in spring; **Brush-tailed Rock-wallabies** peer timidly from the granite boulders above Crows Nest Creek; **Enjoying a picnic by the banks of the creek**, where, if you're quiet and patient, you may be rewarded with a glimpse of one of the park's resident Platypuses.

Western Rim

Rising to 1375 m at **Mount Superbus**, the heavily forested peaks and escarpments of the **Great Dividing Range** form a natural barrier between the coastal lowlands to the east and the rolling hills and plains of the **Darling Downs** to the west. They comprise the western extent of the **Scenic Rim**, that great arc of mountains running from **Gatton** in the north all the way to **Springbrook** in the south.

Cunninghams Gap is the main gateway through the Western Rim. As you climb from the open farmlands of the **Fassifern Valley** you enter a different world: one of rugged mountains, majestic waterfalls, deep gorges and lush rainforest valleys. On the other side of Cunninghams Gap lies the historic town of **Warwick** and the fertile fields of the Darling Downs.

Main Range National Park

Main Range National Park was declared in 1909 in order to preserve the unique mountain environment of the Western Rim. Made up of a series of interconnected sections, it extends from **Mount Mistake** in the north to **Mount Roberts** in the south, taking in other isolated pockets such as **Queen Mary Falls** on the western side of the range. The most easily accessible part of the park is Cunninghams Gap, where there are numerous well-graded walking tracks (ranging from 800 m to 12.4 km return) through the beautiful forests. The 1.4 km (around 25 minutes) **Rainforest Circuit** is particularly delightful.

As the park follows the ridgeline, there are many fine lookouts, including **Mount Mitchell**, **Governor's Chair**, **Sylvester's** and **Fassifern**. The distinctive call of bellbirds can be heard ringing through the trees; also keep an ear out for lyrebirds, which inhabit the rainforest.

Cunninghams Gap is one of two historic passes over the Western Rim (the other is nearby Spicers Gap). It was identified in 1827 by botanist/explorer Allan Cunningham as a possible route over the range. The following year he proved his point by crossing the range here himself. Mt Mitchell towers in the background.

A sense of brooding mystery prevails as the sun sets over the rugged Main Range at Cunninghams Gap.

If you enjoy a mystery, then nearby **Spicers Gap** is a must. Here, hidden in bush, you'll find evidence of the long abandoned pioneering route. The original paved road cut into the mountainside during the mid 1800s is still visible in places, and a pioneer's graveyard marks the final resting place of some early travellers. You can almost hear the sharp crack of the whip and the creaking wheels of laden bullock drays lumbering up the range.

A short detour will take you to **Governor's Chair Lookout**, which gives superb views over the **Fassifern Valley** far below.

Carr's Lookout about 15 km east of Killarney (just beyond Queen Mary Falls) affords great views to the eastern peaks, including:
1. Mount Superbus (1375 m); **2. Wilson's Peak** (1230 m); **3. Mount Barney** (1351 m).

Queen Mary Falls

One of the gems of **Main Range National Park** is beautiful Queen Mary Falls (11 km east of **Killarney**). Here you can take a well-graded 2-km (40 minute) circuit walk through open eucalypt forest to the top of the falls, then down into the lush rainforest gorge and creek below.

This small reserve is host to an amazing variety of wildlife, including the rare Albert's Lyrebird and the equally shy Brush-tailed Rock-wallaby. More common inhabitants include Australian King Parrots, Satin Bowerbirds and Golden Whistlers. You may also see Red Spiny Crayfish in Spring Creek.

Queen Mary Falls, where Spring Creek plunges 40 m down the sheer cliff face into a sheltered rainforest gorge.

Things to See and Do

1   Forest walks, Cunninghams Gap, Main Range NP
2   Old Pioneers' Road, Spicers Gap, Main Range NP
3   Governor's Chair Lookout, Main Range NP
4   Queen Mary Falls circuit walk
5   Lookouts at Mount French, Moogerah Peaks NP
6   Lower Portals pools, Mount Barney NP

Rainforest Residents

The diverse habitats of Main Range National Park provide a home for a great variety of plants and animals, some of them rare (including the Eastern Bristlebird and Coxen's Fig Parrot). More common but still elusive is the Superb Lyrebird (*below left:* a male with his distinctive lyre-shaped tail plumage), whose calls ring with extraordinary clarity

through the rainforest. Adept mimickers, the lyrebird's repertoire includes a host of bird calls and also various mechanical noises such as chainsaws, car horns, and even the sound of tent pegs being driven into the ground!

Another hard-to-find inhabitant is the nocturnal Sugar Glider (*above right*), which can be spotted at night gliding swiftly from tree to tree in search of eucalyptus and acacia sap supplemented by the odd insect or two for protein.

Moogerah Peaks National Park

Moogerah Peaks National Park (just east of the Cunningham Highway near Fassifern) is made up of four separate volcanic mountains – **Mounts French**, **Edwards**, **Greville** and **Moon** – which rise dramatically above the surrounding countryside, cradling **Lake Moogerah**. Mount French is renowned for its impressive cliffs for rock climbing; it also has wheelchair-accessible lookouts at its summit, where you'll enjoy panoramic views of the **Fassifern Valley**, **Tamborine**, **Lamington** and **Mount Barney**.

The park offers many picnicking and walking opportunities, with a range of walks to suit all tastes and levels of fitness. Bird-watchers will be rewarded with sightings of brush-turkeys, finches and Pale-headed Rosellas.

Mount Barney National Park

The rugged mountains of Mount Barney National Park form part of the majestic Scenic Rim and contain some of the largest areas of undisturbed natural habitat in South-East Queensland. Exploration of the park is largely restricted to experienced and well-prepared hikers, as most of the trails are unmarked. There are a few graded walks, however, with the **Lower Portals track** (3.7 km/1.5 hrs one way) leading to a delightful pool (known as Lower Portals) on Mount Barney Creek. Here bottlebrushes and she-oaks line the banks. If observant, you may see the blue flash of a kingfisher as it plunges into a pool to search for dinner.

Right, top to bottom: **Mount Greville** is one of the four volcanic mountains that make up Moogerah Peaks National Park; Many-peaked **Mount Barney** has special significance to three tribes of Aboriginal people; The cliffs of **Mount Maroon** (Mount Barney National Park) dominate the surrounding rural landscape.

Warwick has many fine Victorian-era houses and grand public buildings.

Grafton St, Warwick, retains much of its original charm.

The Imperial Hotel (1905), Warwick, with the lace ironwork so characteristic of this period.

Yangan School of Arts (1897) Yangan is a pretty hamlet on the Settler's Route Tourist Drive.

Warwick

Located 167 km from Brisbane on the western side of the Main Range, Warwick is the primary commercial and agricultural centre serving the **Southern Downs**. The town is famed for its fine colonial architecture, the glorious floral displays of the **Rose Festival**, and the rough-riding antics of jackaroos and jillaroos testing their mettle at the **Warwick Rodeo**. For this reason Warwick is popularly dubbed the "Rose and Rodeo City".

Rose and Rodeo Festival

Without a doubt the most exciting month in Warwick's calendar is October, when the town holds its annual Rose and Rodeo Festival. During the entire month a wide variety of roses are showcased in the city's public (and private) parks and gardens, including Warwick's own specially bred variety, the red "City of Warwick" or Arafuto Rose.

Roses adorn the city of Warwick during the annual Rose and Rodeo Festival.

The culmination of the month's celebrations is the Warwick Rodeo, which lays claim to being one of Australia's oldest and most prestigious rough-riding events. It traces its roots as far back as 1857, when a professional buckjumping contest was held at nearby Canning Downs station.

From Squatter's Run to City

Canning Downs plays an important role in the history of Warwick and the area in general. Attracted by Allan Cunningham's favourable account of the broad plains to the west of the Great Divide, brothers Patrick and George Leslie made their way to the Darling Downs to establish their Canning Downs run in 1840.

Warwick Town Hall (1888) and Criterion Hotel (1917), Palmerin Street.

Canning Downs was the first European settlement outside of Brisbane and soon became an important centre. Just seven years later, the site for the new town was selected on the Canning Downs run. It was to be called Canningtown, until "Warwick" was chosen.

Warwick Post Office (1891) The statue is Thomas Byrnes, Warwick boy and one-time Premier of Queensland.

Boom Town

The town grew rapidly, and, like Toowoomba to the north, the arrival of the railway in 1871 resulted in an economic boom. In the late 19th century a large number of elegant buildings were constructed, mostly from local sandstone. These include the **Court House** (1885), **Masonic Hall** (1886), **Town Hall** (1888), **Police Station** (1890), **National Hotel** (1890) and the **Post Office** (1891). **The Criterion Hotel** (1917), with its superb latticed balconies, is a slightly younger, though no less impressive, building.

Following in the Early Settlers' Footsteps

The perfect way to explore more of the area's heritage is on the **Settler's Route Tourist Drive**. This 72 km round trip takes you from Warwick to **Killarney** and back via the tiny historic settlements of **Yangan**, **Emu Vale**, and **Tannymorel**. From lovely Killarney it's well worth making the short detour (via **Queen Mary Falls**) up to **Carr's Lookout** on the Scenic Rim.

Stanthorpe – Tin Town

Located just 60 km south of Warwick, Stanthorpe is the attractive regional centre of the Granite Belt. A late developer by local standards, the town arose in the 1870s as a result of the discovery of tin in the area, giving rise to its name: "stannum" being Latin for tin, and "thorpe" from the old English word meaning village.

Unlike nearby Warwick, Stanthorpe's architecture is quite modest, with the Post Office (*right*) being the grandest building in town. Also worthwhile is the short trip up to Mount Marley Lookout (*below*) where you'll be rewarded with great views over the town and surrounding countryside.

The Granite Belt

Travel south from Warwick on the **New England Highway** and, within a short distance, the scenery is transformed as you enter the rocky landscape of the Granite Belt. The reason for the moniker soon becomes clear when impressive granite tors appear on either side of the road. The rolling hillsides seem to be peppered with outcrops of stone. In some places these tors are breathtaking in their proportions, towering above the trees or stacked on top of one another like giant marbles poised to tumble.

The Granite Belt is cool climate country, with elevations ranging between 800–1000 m above sea level. Temperatures can drop below freezing in winter – a far cry from the usual subtropical climes of South-East Queensland. Snow even occasionally falls here! These are ideal conditions for viticulture, and, thanks largely to the efforts of Italian POWs and immigrants after WWII, the region is well regarded for its wines. There are more than fifty vineyards in the area surrounding the Granite Belt's main town, **Stanthorpe**, and these provide ample tasting opportunities at the cellar door.

The climate also favours a host of other fruits, with orchards producing apples, pears, peaches, apricots, nectarines and plums, among others. Remember to leave space in your car boot for a boxful of freshly picked produce.

Apple and Grape Harvest Festival, Stanthorpe Australia's leading harvest festival is a three-day celebration in March that pays homage to the region's wine and fruit-growing success. The Granite Belt is renowned for its fresh produce and quality table wines, and visitors to the festival have the opportunity to sample the best produce the region has to offer. Featuring a Grand Parade that showcases a cornucopia of produce, a multicultural fair, the Wine and Food Fiesta, a Gala Ball and a spectacular fireworks display, the festival is the not-to-be-missed social event of the season.

Granite Belt Parks

In addition to its culinary delights, the Granite Belt is famous for its remarkable landscape. The best scenery is to be found in the area's two national parks, **Girraween** (35 km south-east of Stanthorpe) and **Sundown** (79 km south-west of Stanthorpe). Each has unique qualities, but both guarantee a wonderful bushland experience in a superb setting.

Girraween National Park

The more accessible of the two parks, Girraween, which means "place of flowers", is well titled. In springtime the undergrowth becomes a riot of colour as an incredible array of wildflowers bloom amid the granite boulders. The park is also home to a multitude of wildlife, including more than 146 species of birds, making it a favourite haunt for ornithologists.

Girraween is equally renowned for its huge granite tors and outcrops, including the aptly-named **Balancing Rock**, **Sphinx Rock**, **Turtle Rock** and **The Pyramids**. The Pyramids and **Castle Rock** can be climbed and provide excellent 360-degree views over the park and surrounding farmland.

Bushwalking is also a favourite activity, with 17 km of walking tracks in the park. They range from a pleasant 1.5 km (30 minute) circuit to the **Granite Arch**, through to a 10.4 km (approximately 6 hours) return walk to the summit of **Mount Norman** (1267 m) for the more hardy visitor. Other less demanding but highly rewarding walks include **The Pyramids Track** (3 km return, 1.5–2 hours); the **Junction Track** (5 km return, 2.5 hours); and **Castle Rock Track** (3 km return, 1.5–2 hours).

The Boronia is one of the many wildflowers that bring the forest to life with colour in springtime.

Sphinx Rock, Girraween National Park The violent, volcanic past of Girraween National Park is echoed in the unusual rock formations that jut from the park's landscape.

The park has excellent facilities including a **Visitor Centre** (open 7 days a week ranger's duties permitting, Ph: 07 4684 5157), two camping areas with hot showers (booking is advisable, especially in peak periods), and a lovely picnic area on the banks of Bald Rock Creek near the Visitor Centre. Bush camping is allowed by permit obtained prior to your arrival.

During the school holidays you can also enjoy a ranger-led slide show, night-time spotlight tour or a guided walk.

Girraween National Park Graded walking tracks from the Visitor Centre take bushwalkers to impressive rock formations, boulder-strewn creeks and cool waterholes, such as Dr Roberts Waterhole. Dawn and late afternoon are the best times to view wildlife around the park's many water courses and billabongs.

Sundown National Park

In contrast to Girraween's distinctive granite tors, Sundown's landscape is markedly different, being born of a different geological history. Here the predominant rock is sedimentary, meaning that Sundown isn't strictly a Granite Belt park although the nearby intrusions that formed Girraween played their part in the Sundown story.

Sundown is characterised by rugged hills with sharp ridges and peaks deeply incised in places by steep-sided gorges. The most dominant landscape feature is the **Severn River** valley, which cuts its way through the middle of the park and is enclosed at times by sheer slopes. Other highlights are **Red Rock Falls** (a 100-m waterfall after rain), **Red Rock Gorge**, **Mount Lofty** and the curiously named **Rat's Castle** (a granite dyke).

Things to See and Do

1. Sample wine at the local vineyards
2. Photograph spring wildflowers, Girraween NP
3. Take The Pyramids walk, Girraween NP
4. See Red Rock Gorge and Falls, Sundown NP
5. Visit Rat's Castle, Sundown NP

Girraween's Cool Customers

With its high elevation and consequently cool, seasonal climate, Girraween National Park supports a number of plants and animals not normally seen elsewhere in Queensland. These include Flannel Flowers (which you'll find in the Australian Alps nearly 900 km to the south), as well as the Wallangarra White Gum, Superb Lyrebird, Common Wombat (*below right*), Spotted-tailed Quoll, and the rare Turquoise Parrot.

The park is also well-regarded for its abundant birdlife, including numerous honeyeaters (White-eared, Yellow-faced, and Yellow-tufted Honeyeaters), the Buff-rumped Thornbill, and many pretty wrens, including the Superb Fairy-wren (*left*), White-browed Scrubwren, Chestnut-rumped Heathwren, and Southern Emu-wren.

Sundown's vegetation is mainly woodland made up of box, ironbark and cypress, with river red gums, river oaks and tea trees growing along the **Severn River**. Dry vine scrubs are found in the more sheltered gorges.

The park seems a particular favourite for macropods, with wallaroos, Eastern Grey Kangaroos, and mobs of wallabies (Red-necked, Swamp, Brush-tailed Rock and Whiptail) all present here.

Sundown National Park The rugged terrain of Sundown National Park makes it difficult to experience the park's grandeur without a four-wheel-drive, but once there, the sheer cliffs carpeted with forests of eucalypts are truly awe-inspiring.

In addition to its interesting natural history, the park has a fascinating cultural heritage. Originally comprising a number of sheep stations, the cleared areas and yards belong to an earlier pastoral era. You will also find old mine workings scattered about the park, where tin, copper and arsenic were mined sporadically from the 1870s.

Also in contrast to Girraween, Sundown is largely an undeveloped park, with only basic facilities and few marked walking tracks. The main campground is at **The Broadwater**, where there are pit toilets and fireplaces. This southern part of the park is accessible to two-wheel-drive vehicles, but four-wheel-drive is required to explore the northern section.

The Spotted Bowerbird of Sundown NP decorates his nest with little white treasures like stones and bottle caps.

South of Brisbane

Tucked into the very corner of South-East Queensland is the glamour and glitter of one of Australia's best-known holiday playgrounds – the Gold Coast, so named for its golden beaches and sunshine. With a yearly average temperature of 23°C and almost 300 clear, sunny days, the coast attracts visitors from around the world. Once a string of isolated seaside villages with stretches of untouched shores between them, today the 57 km strip of coast from The Spit at Southport to the New South Wales border is one big, bold and racy city, a place geared for holiday enjoyment and relaxation centred on sand, surf and sun. In the mountains and valleys behind the Coast you'll find a hinterland of natural wonders.

Rainbow Lorikeets

Gold Coast

The city of the Gold Coast is long and narrow, sandwiched between the beaches and the hinterland mountains. It is a city that thrives on tourism, international business and commerce, but is also home to nearly 500,000 people. Along the beachfronts tower high-rise holiday apartments, hotels, shops, restaurants, bars and nightclubs, all seeming to be jostling for the best position close to the ocean, making the most of the sea breezes and sunshine. Up and down the beaches there are swimmers, surfers, kiteboarders, sunbathers and walkers who, for their stay on the Gold Coast, leave the workaday world behind and enjoy themselves.

Behind the beachfront strip is the city's business hub – shopping centres, car dealerships, service industries, schools, hospitals, medical centres and the city administration. Beyond lies the sprawl of suburbia, where those who live on the coast relax away from the busy city whose existence depends largely on the many tourists who flock to holiday by the sea.

Hinterland and Rainforest Parks

Away from crowds on the beaches and the busy streets of the coastal strip is an unspoilt tract of pretty hinterland within easy daytrip distance of the coast.

Lamington National Park The park boasts 20,000 ha of subtropical rainforest.

As you leave the coast, great mountains loom in the distance. The first is **Springbrook**, beyond are the **Beechmont and Lamington Plateaus**, divided from Springbrook by the **Numinbah Valley**. The third is **Mount Tamborine**, to the north. All have national parks with cool rainforest and misty waterfalls, and all have spectacular views over the hinterland and the Gold Coast.

As you drive along the winding mountain roads of the hinterland you'll encounter forests, farmland, pretty towns, resorts, restaurants, cabins, wineries and galleries.

Top to bottom: **Main Beach; Marina Mirage; Surfers Paradise; windsurfers** The waters of the Pacific Ocean are great for water sports and sailing.

Chalahn Falls, Lamington National Park Just one of many pretty waterfalls gracing the park.

Gold Coast Beaches and Resorts

Castles Made of Sand

Each year, millions of tourists throng to the Gold Coast to enjoy surfing, swimming, sunbathing or building sandcastles, yet few realise that the Gold Coast itself is built on sand! Even the soaring skyscrapers of Surfers Paradise, Main Beach and Broadbeach stand on sand that 120,000 years ago, during the last ice age, was once the ocean floor when the coast was several kilometres further inland.

The beaches of the Gold Coast sweep in a great arc from **The Spit** in the north to **Coolangatta**. The northern beaches – **Main Beach, Surfers Paradise, Broadbeach, Mermaid, Nobby, Miami, North Burleigh** and **Burleigh** – are the best known, but not to be outdone are the beaches south of Burleigh Head, which curve to the south-east through **Palm Beach, Currumbin, Bilinga Beach, North Kirra, Kirra, Coolangatta** and **Greenmount** to Point Danger. From almost any vantage point the beaches stretch in a seemingly endless curve in both directions. During the day you can enjoy the warm sunshine while marvelling at the sparkling sand, surf and high-rise buildings lining the beaches. Towards sunset, as the beaches darken, the buildings reflect the late afternoon light. When the sun goes down, the coast lights up, and the entire beachfront shimmers with illumination as lights shine from thousands of windows.

The skyline of the northern end of the Gold Coast may be less impressive, but the area is blessed with natural beauty around **Nerang River, South Stradbroke Island** and the **Southport Broadwater**. In the central strip, **Burleigh Head, Tallebudgera Creek, Currumbin Hill** and **Currumbin Creek** make up nature's bounty, while in the south are Greenmount, Point Danger and the **Tweed River**.

Top to bottom: **Sailing on the Broadwater; Main Beach at sunrise; The view from Southport to Main Beach.**

South Stradbroke Island

The low sand island of South Stradbroke is the smaller sibling of South-East Queensland's large sand islands to the north. Long ocean beaches and quiet coves enhance the island's secluded beauty. Most of the island is a conservation park and bountiful wildlife inhabits the casuarina and banksia scrub. Mangroves on the Broadwater side also shelter various marine species. Mid-way up the island on the Broadwater side is **Couran Cove**, an eco-resort just a short boat ride from the heart of the Gold Coast. The waters behind South Stradbroke Island provide boat access to **Paradise Point, Sanctuary Cove** and **Runaway Bay** at the mouth of the **Coomera River**.

Sovereign Island Located just off Paradise Point, Sovereign Island is now one of the coast's most prestigious addresses.

Sanctuary Cove Giftware shops, upmarket restaurants and antique stores line the streets.

Sensational Sea World

Sea World, on The Spit at Main Beach, is one of the Gold Coast's premier tourist attractions. The theme park is a fun-filled mix of close encounters with sea creatures, thrilling rides and roller-coasters, and entertainment and wildlife shows including the Dolphin Cove Show, Quest for the Golden Seal and Waterski WipeOut. See Polar bears (*right*) frolic in their specially built Arctic summer playground Polar Bear Shores, come face to face with the ocean's most feared predators at Shark Bay, or watch penguins, seals, dolphins and dugong.

Sea World is open every day from 10 a.m.–5 p.m., closed Christmas Day and half day Anzac Day. Ph: 07 5588 2205 for entry fee.

Southport and Main Beach

In the 19th century, **Southport** was the biggest town on the south coast, but, as **Surfers Paradise** grew in popularity to become the mecca for Queensland tourism, the older town was left in its shadow, remaining a sleepy seaside retreat with a small business centre on the **Broadwater**. **Main Beach**, across the Broadwater at the southern end of **The Spit**, was little more than a few holiday houses nestling behind the **Southport Surf Lifesaving Club**. In recent times all this has changed. Hotels, marinas and the **Sea World** theme park have turned The Spit and Broadwater into a colourful entertainment precinct that attracts visitors by the bus load. Southport has been reinvented as a modern shopping and business centre, and high-rise holiday apartment buildings are springing up all along the Broadwater to the north. Main Beach now has a forest of high-rise apartments rivalling that of Surfers Paradise.

The Broadwater is a well-loved anchorage for the coast's many boating and water sports enthusiasts. This safe harbour is close to world-class shops and restaurants, yet still within easy reach of the ocean for diving and deep-water fishing. At Southport, picnic facilities and waterfront promenades along The Broadwater foreshore make it one of the Gold Coast's most delightful places to sit and watch the boats sailing past.

1. Sheraton Mirage 2. Palazzo Versace 3. Marina Mirage 4. Riverside Centre 5. Surfers Paradise 6. Main Beach 7. Broadwater 8. Lamington Plateau 9. Southport

On the Broadwater's opposite side is **Marina Mirage**, with its distinctive sail-like roof standing out against the eastern skyline and mirroring the Broadwater's masts and sails. Here too are the **Palazzo Versace** and **Sheraton Mirage** resort hotels, **Sea World** and the **Sea World Nara Resort**. The whole of the 4 km ocean stretch of The Spit, from Main Beach to the **Gold Coast Seaway**, is natural casuarina-covered dunes with walkways, picnic areas and beach access points. You can enjoy a view uninterrupted by imposing apartment buildings, while still being close to the glitter and shopping of Main Beach, Surfers Paradise and Broadbeach.

At **Labrador**, to Southport's north, much of the shoreline is boardwalk and parkland with views across the Broadwater to the Seaway, where deep-sea fishing charter boats head out to the Pacific Ocean. At low tide, the large, bare **Wavebreak Island** is exposed and boats must follow the channels closely. Further north, around the **Coomera River** mouth, are canal estates and residential suburbs.

Left to right: **Broadwater from the Spit; Main Beach; Main Beach surf patrol** The northern end of the Gold Coast now rivals the glamour of destinations such as Surfers Paradise, Broadbeach, Burleigh and Coolangatta. Southport was one of the original holiday towns of South-East Queensland before the area came to be called the Gold Coast. Southport, The Broadwater, The Spit and Main Beach were popular holiday resorts when Surfers Paradise and Broadbeach were little more than sand dunes and shacks. At that time, the beaches of Burleigh and Coolangatta were considered a long way away; now, all are just an easy train ride from Brisbane.

Surfers Paradise

Back in the 1920s, a Brisbane hotelier named Jim Cavill bought 10 ha of beachfront land at a place called Elston, where Surfers Paradise stands. The land was very much like the undeveloped part of The Spit today – dunes carpeted with casuarinas and dune grass, an unspoiled golden beach leading into swampy, sandy mud flats and mangroves behind to the **Nerang River**.

Today, the name Elston doesn't appear in the Gold Coast street directory, but Cavill is the name of the mall that is the heart of Surfers Paradise. A few years before Cavill bought his land and built a hotel he called the Cavill, a Brisbane real estate firm tried, surprisingly unsuccessfully, to auction land they described as "Surfers Paradise Estate". Cavill liked the name and his efforts to have the name Elston changed to Surfers Paradise were successful in 1933. By then a bridge had been built over the Nerang River at Southport and the road from Brisbane to Southport was extended to Surfers Paradise and further, sparking the tourism boom that continues throughout the Gold Coast and its hinterland.

Early development was along the beachfront but the original buildings have given way to high-rise hotels and apartment buildings that are now as synonymous with Surfers Paradise as the famous, golden-bikini-clad "Meter Maids" that patrol the streets. Since the 1960s, the low-lying land behind Surfers Paradise has been transformed into vast, often luxurious, canal estates – another of the coast's identifying features. At Surfers Paradise you can treat yourself to ocean views from tall holiday apartments – one reaches 78 levels! – rising above opulent hotels, gourmet restaurants, throbbing nightclubs and boutique shops arranged along 4 km of beautiful, landscaped beachfront.

Surfers Paradise Beach The golden beach fronts some equally golden real estate. The land on which the high-rise hotels and apartments of Surfers Paradise stand is some of the most valuable real estate in Australia.

Paths and park benches above the beach provide relaxing spots to watch the surf crash in. You'll share this colourful and relaxed place with thousands of holidaymakers – by day, strolling the malls and shops, wandering the esplanade or beaches, dining in the sidewalk cafés and lazing in the sun and surf; by night, you can mix and mingle with people from around the globe in the many excellent restaurants, trendy bars and thumping late-night clubs.

Labelled a paradise for surfers almost a century ago, today it is a paradise for many other reasons, almost all of which involve having a good time!

Surfers Paradise, looking south along the Gold Coast Highway Surfers Paradise has one of Australia's highest population densities and is one of the nation's most visited tourist destinations. Tourists and residents alike enjoy high-rise living and sea views.

Beach arch at Surfers Paradise Esplanade A large golden arch is a fitting welcome to Surfers Paradise. Beyond the arch is a wide stairway leading to the sands and waves that give the holiday playground its name.

Esplanade The Esplanade at Surfers Paradise, dominated by tall Norfolk Island pines, is the perfect place to stroll along the shady, tree-lined paths, or to sit and watch surfers, windsurfers and kiteboarders at play.

Indy Fever

In October each year Surfers Paradise reverberates to the roar of high-speed racing cars when the Indy Carnival hits town, turning streets into a motor-racing circuit by day and initiating rounds of partying by night.

The racing centres on the American Champ Cars, the no-holds-barred open-wheelers, and the Australian-bred V8 Supercars. Over four days these machines speed around the tight street circuit among the apartment towers and along the beach front as they compete in testing and practice races before contesting the main events.

Broadbeach

Once overshadowed by Surfers Paradise, Broadbeach is now the focal point for Gold Coast entertainment. **Jupiters Casino**, **Conrad Jupiters Hotel**, the **Gold Coast Convention Centre** and **Pacific Fair Shopping Centre** entice visitors to this busy enclave on the waterways of the Nerang River.

In the 1940s and 50s, the dunes between today's Gold Coast Highway and Broadbeach were mined for mineral sands. When mining ceased, the land was rejuvenated with grasses and trees and auctioned for development. In 1957, Lennons Broadbeach Hotel, an eight-storey block standing seemingly in the middle of nowhere, was built on the land. But the hotel, now long demolished, was to spark a development boom that continues today, making Broadbeach a thriving seaside resort and residential area with well-developed foreshore parks and beach facilities.

Behind Surfers Paradise and Broadbeach are some of the Gold Coast's major sporting facilities. At Bundall, January brings the Gold Coast Turf Club's prestigious horse-racing carnival and yearling thoroughbred sales, dubbed the **Magic Millions**. Behind Broadbeach, three of the Coast's premier golf courses – **Royal Pines Resort, Palm Meadows and Emerald Lakes** – invite professionals and novices. Further south are six more golf courses – **Surfers Paradise, Merrimac public course, Lakelands, Paradise Springs, Gold Coast Burleigh** and **Robina Woods**. For those who prefer boisterous sports thronging with fans, the **Indy 300** is a must-see event.

Left to right: **Pacific Fair; Raptis Plaza, Cavill Mall; Mikado** Pacific Fair, behind Broadbeach, is one of the Gold Coast's largest shopping centres. In the heart of Surfers Paradise are the Raptis Plaza in the Cavill Mall and the Mikado Japanese Restaurant at the corner of Elkhorn Avenue and the Gold Coast Highway. Gold Coast architecture, whether it is for community facilities and public buildings, hotels, restaurants or the dominant skyscraper apartment buildings that crowd the shoreline, defines the holiday atmosphere that centres on light, breezy entertainment and a good time day and night.

Top to bottom: Beach patrol; Fun on the beach; Rainbow Lorikeets frequent the area; Competitors dash for the sea in a surf carnival.

Burleigh Heads and Burleigh Beach

The chain of beaches from The Spit at Southport in the north to Coolangatta in the south is broken only by two creeks and a major headland, Burleigh Head. The headland from which the suburb of Burleigh Heads takes its name was originally called *Jellurgul* by Aboriginal inhabitants before being renamed Burly Head in 1940 by a surveyor because of its massive appearance. Over time the spelling changed to Burleigh. This great basalt bluff carpeted in greenery is a bulwark against the waves, a natural groyne on the north side of **Tallebudgera Creek** that creates the beaches sweeping away to the north. Without Burleigh Head the shoreline would be further back and Broadbeach and Surfers Paradise – and perhaps The Spit and South Stradbroke Island – would not contain the stunning beaches they do today. Burleigh Head and its smaller namesake, **Little Burleigh** (sometimes called North Burleigh or South Nobby), create the beautiful beach foreshore, breaking the southerly and south-easterly winds that blow regularly and making the beaches sheltered and safer for swimming.

Burleigh Heads is a quieter part of the Gold Coast with fewer high-rise buildings than Surfers Paradise, Broadbeach or Coolangatta. Yet it has all the requirements for a top holiday spot. As well as finding superb beaches, you'll enjoy a foreshore graced with shady trees, lawns and pathways along **The Esplanade** running parallel to the beach. There are shops and restaurants, a caravan park, blocks of holiday accommodation and apartment buildings on the lower northern slopes of Burleigh Head.

Behind Burleigh Heads is **Burleigh Waters**, the southernmost of the canal and lake estates that converge with similar inland waterways to the north at **Mermaid Waters** and **Broadbeach Waters**. These canals are perfectly pleasant for boating, but are unsafe for swimming as they are frequented by sharks.

Top to bottom: Burleigh Beach; Burleigh Beach, from Little Burleigh; Burleigh Head The beach is one of the most popular on the Gold Coast.

Tallebudgera

Immediately south of Burleigh Heads is **Tallebudgera Creek**, which flows from the mountains of **Springbrook National Park**. As its lower reaches meet the sea, the creek broadens into a wide, tidal waterway with a sandy southern shore that is perfect for canoeing, boating and swimming. Near the creek mouth on the southern side is the **Tallebudgera Recreation Camp**, a long-time venue for school physical fitness camps. The camp has direct access to Tallebudgera Creek and the ocean beach, allowing for a range of water sports.

Burleigh Heads and Tallebudgera Creek are important natural areas as they include **Burleigh Ridge Park** and **Tallebudgera Creek Conservation Park**, near which is another of Queensland's excellent animal sanctuaries, **David Fleay Wildlife Park**. Burleigh Ridge Park and **Burleigh Head National Park** both make up significant Koala habitat in a corridor of greenery which is, unfortunately for its marsupial residents, divided by the Gold Coast Highway.

Burleigh Head National Park

About 20 million years ago when Mount Warning was an active volcano, one of its lava flows reached the sea at Burleigh and solidified into a basalt mass that is now Burleigh Head. As the lava slowly cooled, shrinkage caused it to form six-sided columns called columnar basalt. These columns, some up to 1 m in diameter can be seen in the rocky cliff faces of Burleigh Head and lying broken at its base, where the waves have eroded them over millions of years.

The headland is blanketed with diverse vegetation types and is a refuge for plant and animal species, some considered rare. It has a valuable example of "littoral rainforest" – a dry form of rainforest that grows only near the sea. The complex vegetation of the littoral rainforest thrives in the rich, dark soil that slowly covered the headland as the basalt decomposed. Eucalypt species, including brush box, ironbark, bloodwood and forest red gum grow in the poorer soils. Pandanus groves and a small pocket of coastal heath flourish on the exposed seaward slopes.

You may be lucky enough to see Koalas in the forest red gums, and sightings of brush-turkeys are common. Also seen are White-bellied Sea-Eagles, Brahminy Kites, Whistling Kites, Ospreys and many species of fruit-eating parrots. The headland is a feeding ground for migratory birds.

Surf Carnivals and Events

On almost any weekend through summer you can watch teams of bronzed surf lifesavers competing in swimming events, beach races, rescue competitions and spectacular surf boat racing on the Gold Coast's main beaches.

Although rescue of swimmers in trouble in the surf is today usually done by surf ski or jet ski, the traditional big wooden surf boats rowed by lifesavers are still used in competition. At Surfers Paradise, a statue commemorates Peter Lacey, a four-time world championship winner.

Little Burleigh Head looking north to Surfers Paradise.

Walking Burleigh Head

A walk along the shade-dappled tracks of **Burleigh Head National Park** is an uplifting natural experience on the highly developed Gold Coast. Here you can walk over and around an almost untouched headland that is preserved as a national park.

Walking tracks start near the Gold Coast Highway on the southern side of the headland or above the beach on the northern side.

You have a choice of easy or steep-grade tracks passing through rainforest over the headland, or around its base above the tumbled and broken basalt columns where waves crash below. Spectacular views take in the ocean, the beachfront up to **Surfers Paradise**, and **Tallebudgera Creek** down to **Point Danger**.

Below: **Burleigh Head National Park** Views from this wild, magnificent headland are stunning.

Palm Beach and Currumbin

Palm Beach lies between the two creeks that flow to sea on the southern Gold Coast – **Tallebudgera Creek** and **Currumbin Creek**. Palm Beach is primarily a residential and holiday-home suburb along a 4 km stretch of beach between the two creeks. The beach is defined by Burleigh Head in the north and Currumbin Hill in the south. The southern part of the beach runs to an area of casuarina-covered sand dunes and a bare sand spit to an artificial rock groyne on the northern side of the Currumbin Creek mouth. Behind the dunes is a quiet lagoon off the creek, flanked on the western side by more dunes and bushland.

The land behind Palm Beach was first settled as a cattle grazing property in the late 19th century. Although a railway line linked Brisbane with Southport and Coolangatta by 1903, the route was well west of the beach areas and most people bypassed the beaches of the central Gold Coast. But when roads were built down the coastal strip and cars came into general use, places like Palm Beach and Currumbin became popular holiday destinations.

Today Palm Beach is a large and growing suburb extending inland to **Elanora** and **Reedy Creek**, and towards the foothills of **Springbrook** in the hinterland.

Palm Beach and Currumbin Creek The southern end of Palm Beach and the mouth of Currumbin Creek with the suburbs of the southern Gold Coast and hinterland mountains in the distance.

Currumbin estuary and beach Currumbin Rock (foreground) creates the southern side of the Currumbin Creek mouth. An artificial groyne has been built behind the rock to prevent waves breaking through and blocking up the creek's mouth with sand. Behind is Currumbin Hill, home of Currumbin Sanctuary. Down the beach is the jagged outcrop of Elephant Rock near the Currumbin Surf Lifesaving Club.

Elephant Rock at Currumbin looking north The flush of dawn over the Surfers Paradise skyline, which looms behind Elephant Rock, sited about a kilometre south of Currumbin Creek.

Currumbin

On the creek's southern side are Currumbin and **Currumbin Valley**; farms were established here in the late 19th century, making these some of the earliest settled areas on the southern coast. Today Currumbin is a prime holiday area where the Gold Coast Highway, which snakes down through the beachside areas from Southport, meets the Pacific Highway, the main north-south route through the Coast's western areas.

Currumbin is dominated by **Currumbin Hill**, which is part conservation park and home to the National Trust's **Currumbin Wildlife Sanctuary**, famous for its birds, especially Rainbow Lorikeets, which flock to be fed by visitors.

Currumbin Wildlife Sanctuary

Currumbin Sanctuary, a 27 ha bushland park tucked under Currumbin Hill, is home to one of the world's largest collections of Australian native animals.

In a bush setting you can see more than 1400 mammals, birds and reptiles including Koalas, kangaroos, snakes, crocodiles and Rainbow Lorikeets, which you can also feed by hand (*below*).

The Sanctuary, established as a private enterprise in the 1950s by Alex Griffiths, is now operated as a tourist park and research facility by the National Trust of Queensland. Open daily except Christmas Day and from 1 p.m. Anzac Day. Ph: 07 5534 1266 for entry fee.

Currumbin Valley

Currumbin marks the start of an adventurous trip into the southern Gold Coast hinterland. The Currumbin Valley Road follows **Currumbin Creek** up towards the mountains of the **McPherson Range** and into historic and beautiful landscape.

In the lovely Currumbin Valley you will come to an area where the road forks, with Currumbin Creek Road to the right and Tomewin-Currumbin Creek Road to the left. Take the Tomewin road and after just a few hundred metres you will discover a small national park – the **Nicoll Scrub National Park** – on the left. Nearly 2 km further into this wild and rugged country you come to the Queensland–New South Wales border, where the road turns south-west to cross the border from the Queensland side. Eventually this road leads past a border gate marking your entry into New South Wales and follows on to the Tomewin area of the **Tweed Valley**. Once a major timber-getting area for red cedar and rosewood, **Tomewin** was also on the old Cobb & Co coach route from **Murwillumbah** to **Nerang**. Just 20 km inland from **Coolangatta**, this elevated, isolated country is more than 300 m above sea level and is dominated by **Mount Tomewin**, 457 m.

A relaxing overnight stay in the Tomewin area can be had at one of the many attractive cabins and homestays, from which you can backtrack the next day to Currumbin, or continue into the Tweed Valley and follow a road through Murwillumbah to Tweed Heads and back to the Gold Coast.

Rocky Pool, Currumbin Valley The Currumbin Valley is a picturesque part of the Gold Coast far from the beaches and buildings. Relax at one of the many roadside picnic spots that dot this secluded valley.

Indigenous Inhabitants

The Indigenous past of the area is evident in the many towns with names of Aboriginal origin, including Currumbin, Tallebudgera and nearby Murwillumbah. Tallebudgera is said to be derived from Aboriginal words meaning "good fish" in the creek. Currumbin is the word for a species of pine common in the area. Murwillumbah means either "place of many possums" or "camp place".

Walking the shore

The foreshores of the Gold Coast's beaches have many kilometres of walking paths through the shady landscaped parks, many with giant Norfolk Island pines planted when the beaches first came to be used for seaside holidays.

Using these walkways, a 36-km path named **Oceanway** has been established between Point Danger and the Gold Coast Seaway.

Coolangatta

In the early years of last century, when a rail line was put in from Brisbane, the Gold Coast – long before it was even called that! – had just two popular seaside resorts: Southport and Coolangatta. The longer train ride to Coolangatta made it a journey mostly for the young and adventurous, an image Coolangatta retained even when roads began to bring visitors by car to the growing coastal towns. Today, Coolangatta and Tweed Heads (its sister town over the border) possess a character different from the more staid Southport and the glitzy Surfers Paradise and Broadbeach.

From Surfers Paradise, the great curve of beaches to the south, ending with a headland and a cluster of tall apartment buildings, marks Coolangatta with Greenmount Hill and Point Danger beyond. This end of the Gold Coast is a premier place for a seaside holiday and here you'll find good beaches, great surfing, pleasant parks and walks, restaurants, bars, entertainment, galleries and shops.

Above: **Coolangatta and Point Danger, looking west** Point Danger is Queensland's most easterly mainland point. Below the point, to the right, are Snapper Rocks, which help to create one of the best surfing breaks in Australia. Beyond are Rainbow Bay Beach, Greenmount Hill, Greenmount Beach, Coolangatta Beach and Kirra Beach. Left of Point Danger are Duranbah Beach and the Tweed River.

Point Danger

Although Australia's most easterly point is claimed by Cape Byron, 52 km south of the Gold Coast, if you stand on the edge of Point Danger, under the very unconventional lighthouse that stands as a memorial to Captain Cook, you will be on the State's most easterly mainland point.

When facing seaward from Point Danger you can see the vast Pacific Ocean stretching before you. And if you turn around, looking westward, you'll have the whole of Australia at your feet.

Left: **Point Danger Lighthouse** is a memorial to Captain Cook, who sailed past in 1770.

Kirra Beach Foreshore pandanus frame Kirra Beach near the southern end of the Gold Coast.

Kirra Point and Kirra Beach The low headland of Kirra Point creates the sweep of Kirra Beach.

Beautiful Beaches

The sweep of beach from Currumbin Creek to Snapper Rocks promises some of the best swells on the Gold Coast, rolling into small bays that are defined by headlands or rocks. Currumbin has **Currumbin Rock** and **Elephant Rock**. **Tugun Beach** has **Flat Rock** at its northern end and a continuous foreshore down **Tugun**, **Bilinga**, **North Kirra** and **Kirra** beaches to the jutting, rocky, **Kirra Point**.

In between Kirra Point and nearby Greenmount Hill nestle two of the most popular beaches on the Gold Coast, **Coolangatta Beach** and **Greenmount Beach**. A rocky foreshore below Pat Fagan Park on Greenmount Hill shelters the western side of tiny **Rainbow Bay** and Snapper Rocks mark the eastern boundary around to Point Danger. Below Point Danger, curving around to the Tweed River mouth, is **Duranbah Beach**. The parkland on Greenmount Hill around to the top of Point Danger has spectacular views over the ocean and beaches.

Surf's Up

Surfing is a passion on the Gold Coast, and Burleigh Head and Snapper Rocks at Point Danger are two of the best surfing spots.

Pumped sand has formed a bank, named the "Super Bank" by local surfers, that creates excellent waves from the Point to Kirra.

Above, top to bottom: **Surfing and fishing are both popular pastimes on the Gold Coast's many beaches.**

The Tweed River

Boundary Street cuts through the middle of Coolangatta, but it is not your average street – it is also the border between Queensland and New South Wales. Cross to the southern side of the street and you'll find yourself in the northern New South Wales town of Tweed Heads, at the mouth of the Tweed River, just a stone's throw from Queensland.

The Tweed River rises high up in the mountains to the south-west of **Mount Warning**, the volcanic plug of a once massive volcano that 23 million years ago spewed out lava which cooled to create the mountains that encircle the **Tweed Valley** today.

The Tweed River, joined by many creeks and tributaries from the rim of mountains, runs north-easterly past Mount Warning and through the towns of **Murwillumbah**, **Tumbulgum** and **Chindera** to meet the ocean at Tweed Heads.

Encircling the perpetually green Tweed Valley and Mount Warning are lush, rainforest-covered mountains that are protected as national parks. These include **Lamington and Springbrook National Parks** in Queensland and the **Border Ranges** and **Nightcap National Parks** in New South Wales. All are places of great natural beauty with extensive visitor facilities and walking tracks through the mountains.

Right, top to bottom: **Tweed Maritime Museum; Fishing trawlers in the Tweed River** The Tweed River is a major commercial fishing base on Australia's east coast. The river is also a boating and fishing paradise with hundreds of kilometres of safe waterways through the lush countryside of the Tweed River Valley .

Theme Parks and Entertainment

If you're seeking a fun-filled, family day out, the Gold Coast certainly provides. The Coast has two major wildlife parks – the **David Fleay Wildlife Park** and **Currumbin Wildlife Sanctuary** – and four theme parks. All charge an entry fee and are open daily except for Christmas Day and Anzac Day morning.

Big Four Theme Parks

Sea World (see also page 100) is the longest-established of the major theme parks and treats visitors to a wealth of information on marine life and aquatic environments, as well as displays, water slides and rides (Seaworld Drive, Main Beach, The Spit, Ph: 07 5599 2205).

Dreamworld, a giant fairground of entertainment and exotic animal shows, includes Bengal Tigers, Cougars, native animals, and some of the tallest and fastest rides in the world – the Giant Drop, the Tower of Terror and The Claw (Pacific Highway, Oxenford, Ph: 07 5588 1122).

Warner Bros Movie World, billed as "Hollywood on the Gold Coast", is a working movie-making studio and fun park where you can watch staged shows and meet popular cartoon characters (Pacific Highway, Oxenford, Ph: 07 5573 8485).

Nearby **Wet 'n' Wild** is an aquatic fun park featuring a giant waterslide and rides. Take the plunge at Mammoth Falls or ride the Terror Canyon (Pacific Highway, Oxenford, Ph: 07 5573 2255).

Tiger Island, Dreamworld, is one of the park's many drawcards. Here you can watch white and gold Bengal Tigers swim, play and interact with trainers, and you can learn about the efforts being made to conserve and protect these awesome beasts.

Sea World Dolphin Cove Performing dolphins at Dolphin Cove have long been one of Sea World's favourite shows. Sea World is an important player in the conservation of many marine species and its team of veterinarians and handlers carry out important research.

Wet 'n' Wild Speedcoaster Watery fun at Buccaneer Bay is just one of the activities at Wet 'n' Wild at Oxenford. Another attraction is the Super 8 Aqua Racer.

Sylvester about to hug a little girl at Movie World Visitors can mix with larger-than-life cartoon characters and watch staged shows with movie themes, including hair-raising stunts.

David Fleay Wildlife Park

The David Fleay Wildlife Park, on Tallebudgera Creek at West Burleigh, has a large collection of Australian wildlife, many of them rare and threatened species. Naturalist David Fleay founded the park in 1953 and went on to become the first scientist to breed Platypuses successfully in captivity.

Now, the Environmental Protection Agency manages the park as an educational facility to highlight the need for conservation of native animals. You can see cassowaries, Platypuses, Dingos and wallabies displayed in surroundings similar to their native habitat.

Open 9 a.m.–5 p.m. daily, except Christmas Day. Ph: 07 5576 2411 for entry fee.

Other Things to See and Do

As well as the four major theme parks, two additions at Oxenford are **Paradise Country** and the **Australian Outback Spectacular**. Paradise Country (Pacific Motorway, Oxenford, Ph: 07 5573 8270) is a farm experience with activities that reflect bush traditions such as whip cracking, cow milking and sheep mustering, and visitors can enjoy an outback "smoko" of billy tea and damper under a gum tree. The Outback Spectacular (Pacific Motorway, Oxenford, Ph: 07 5573 8315) is a night-time, action-packed performance by riders on stockhorses who play out a story of two rival cattle stations.

Other Gold Coast attractions include boat cruises, go-kart driving, pistol shooting, tenpin bowling, whale watching, charter fishing tours or jet skiing. For the fearless, **bungy jumping**, **parasailing** or **joy flights in a helicopter, open cockpit plane, seaplane or warplane**, provide a real adrenaline rush.

For indoor types, entertainment includes: **Timezone** (Level 1, Centro, Surfers Paradise, Ph: 07 5539 9500); **The Wax Museum** (Cnr Elkhorn & Ferny Aves, Surfers Paradise, Ph: 07 5538 3975); **King Tutt's Egyptian and Dinosaur Adventure** with Putt Putt mini golf (Cnr Gold Coast Hwy and Pandanus Ave, Surfers Paradise, Ph: 07 5570 2277); **Cyberzone Internet Cafe and Gaming Lounge** (Lvl 1, Centro, Surfers Paradise, Ph: 07 5538 0148); **Bungy Australia**, the Coast's only bungy jump (16 Palm Ave, Surfers Paradise, Ph: 07 5570 4833).

The **Gold Coast Arts Centre** (135 Bundall Rd, Surfers Paradise, Ph: 07 5581 6500) also offers live entertainment, films, and art and craft shows.

Every weekend, markets on the coast sell a range of food, art and craft, produce and bric-a-brac. They include **Carrara Country Market** (Saturday & Sunday, Broadbeach–Nerang Rd, Merrimac, Ph: 07 5579 9388); **Broadbeach Art and Craft Market** (1st & 3rd Sunday of each month, Kurrawa Park, Broadbeach, Ph: 07 5533 8202); **Burleigh Heads Market** (last Sunday each month, Marine Pde, Burleigh Heads, Ph: 07 5533 8202); **Coolangatta Markets** (2nd Sunday each month, Marine Pde, Coolangatta, Ph: 07 5533 8202); **Mudgeeraba Village Fair** (1st Saturday each month, Railway St, Mudgeeraba, Ph: 07 5530 3201 or 5525 2845); **Tamborine Markets** (2nd Sunday each month, Showgrounds, Tamborine Mountain, Ph 07 5545 4625).

Ripley's Believe It or Not Museum

Be amazed and bewildered at the Ripley's Believe It or Not Museum as you wander through twelve themed galleries featuring hundreds of unbelievable and mysterious exhibits, including interactive displays, magic tricks and illusions. Open 9 a.m. –11 p.m. daily, Raptis Plaza, Cavill Mall, Surfers Paradise. Ph: 07 5592 0040 for entry fee.

Scenic Rim

The Gold Coast Hinterland is at the south-east corner of the Scenic Rim – a great three-quarter-circle of ranges that starts at the Border Ranges and runs through to Cunninghams Gap and Mount Mistake. It includes Mount Barney and Mount Lindesay.

The Scenic Rim has many national parks and conservation reserves that protect a variety of ecosystems ranging from rainforest to coastal dunes.

Top to bottom: **View to the Gold Coast from Tamborine; Tamborine Botanic Gardens** The Botanic Gardens are a focus of the annual Springtime on the Mountain Festival.

Gold Coast Hinterland

Travelling inland away from the glamour and glitz of the Gold Coast tourist strip, you discover a whole new world. The Gold Coast hinterland is a place of mountains and valleys, of small towns and farms, country roads and picnic grounds. The hinterland includes the slopes and tops of the **Border Ranges**, **Springbrook**, the **Lamington Plateau**, the **Darlington Range**, **Tamborine Mountain** and the valleys of the **Nerang, Coomera, Albert and Logan rivers**. This picturesque area is crisscrossed by roads and highways that make for easy touring from the Gold Coast. Through Nerang, you can head to Springbrook and the Numinbah Valley, Beechmont and the Lamington Plateau, Canungra and Beaudesert, or venture up the Gold Coast Motorway (Exit 57) to **Tamborine Mountain**.

Tamborine Mountain

Nestled on an 8 km-long and 4 km-wide plateau 550 m above sea level, and half-way between the Gold Coast and Brisbane, are the villages of **Tamborine Mountain**, **North Tamborine** and **Eagle Heights**. In this cool, green place flourish thick rainforest and tall eucalypts. Tropical gardens dotted with flowers surround charming homes, and grass grows profusely right up to the edges of the winding mountain roads.

Tamborine Mountain is home to galleries and craft studios, cafés and restaurants, antique shops, wineries and nurseries. And because it is so compact, it is easy to explore simply by strolling from gallery to gallery, tasting wine, dining, relaxing in the parks and picnic areas, and visiting the **Heritage Centre** and **Botanic Gardens**. For those seeking a longer stay, accommodation at Tamborine Mountain has a quaint, peaceful flavour and includes chalets, cabins, cottages, lodges and motels as well as traditional pubs and bed and breakfast homestays.

The entire mountain is a flora and fauna sanctuary where protected wildlife shelters in seven distinct national parks. Pademelons are often seen on the road verges and many species of birdlife, frogs and butterflies inhabit the forests.

Gallery walk More than a dozen galleries, craft, gift and antique shops make the streets of the pretty moutain-top village of Tamborine Mountain well worth a visit.

Palm Grove National Park Thick stands of piccabeen palms grow in the rainforest at the headwaters of Stoney Creek on the eastern side of Mount Tamborine.

Tamborine National Parks

Curtis Falls in Joalah NP Cascading falls on Cedar Creek, which flows from Mount Tamborine, are just a short walk from one of the main roads that leads through the North Tamborine village.

Mount Tamborine is virtually ringed by small but significant national parks. These rainforest parks, grouped under the name Tamborine National Park, also each have their own name and contain in total 22 km of graded walking tracks.

Joalah National Park, located close to the village of North Tamborine, is on **Cedar Creek**, and a 4.2-km circuit track follows the creek's gorge. Other main parks include tiny **Macdonald National Park**, which adjoins the Tamborine Botanic Gardens, **Witches Falls** (the State's first national park, established in 1908) and **The Knoll** on the mountain's north-western side, **Cedar Creek** below the northern slopes, **Palm Grove** on the eastern edge, and **Lepidozamia** in the south.

Violent Origins

The basalt cliffs and outcrops of Mount Tamborine are the most northerly remnant of lava flows from Mount Warning, 55 km to the south, when it was an active volcano about 23 million years ago.

Growing in the rich volcanic soils are patches of subtropical rainforest dominated by tall piccabeen palms. Unusual cycads, relics of plants which flourished almost 150 million years ago, also grow in places on the mountain.

Tamborine's lower slopes have significant areas of more open forest.

Natural History of Tamborine National Park

The rainforest of Tamborine National Park has a large variety of native animals such as the Graceful Tree-frog (*right*) and the Land Mullet, one of the world's largest skinks.

The Richmond Birdwing Butterfly (*left*) is seen frequently, and birdlife includes the rare Albert's Lyrebird, Noisy Pittas, brush-turkeys, Rainbow Lorikeets, bowerbirds and whipbirds. Platypus live in the mountain's creeks and at night fireflies can be seen in the rainforest, and glow-worms at Curtis Falls.

Heritage and History

Prior to European settlement, Tamborine Mountain had an Indigenous population and it is thought that the name Tamborine comes from an Aboriginal word for "place of yams".

Early colonial history of Tamborine Mountain is preserved in the **Heritage Centre** at **Eagle Heights**. Immigrants, many of them Irish, came to the area in the 1860s and the first leases of land were taken up in 1875.

You can visit the centre's historic buildings, which include a dairy and a blacksmith shop, or see old wagons and farm machinery. A Pioneer Hall includes a diorama depicting the early timber industry, when timbergetters ventured up into the mountain's forests in the mid-19th century looking for prized cedar and beech as well as eucalypts. The Heritage Centre is open from 11 a.m. to 3 p.m. each Sunday (Ph: 07 5545 1904).

Right: **Tamborine Mountain Heritage Centre** Buildings from the early settlement era, such as a general store *(top)* and a slab hut *(bottom)*, have been preserved at the Heritage Centre.

Purling Brook Falls plunge into Springbrook National Park.

Morans Falls are situated near O'Reilly's Rainforest Guesthouse.

116

Border Ranges

Some of Australia's wildest and most rugged mountain country lies in a great swathe along the eastern sector of the border between Queensland and New South Wales. Here, you find the Border Ranges, a place of high, rainforest-covered mountains and plateaus, lines of ridges and cliffs, deep gorges, and plunging waterfalls – most in their natural state and preserved as national park. The ranges were formed out of massive lava flows from **Mount Warning** when it was an active volcano. When the lava solidified and cooled, primitive plants took root, beginning an ecosystem that grew into the complex subtropical rainforest that blankets the mountain tops and valleys. Today's rainforests of **Lamington National Park** and **Springbrook** are survivors of an era when rainforest covered most of Australia and the climate was wetter and cooler. As the climate became hotter and drier, the cool temperate rainforests were limited to areas where the climate was still favourable, such as Lamington and Springbrook and the **Border Ranges National Park** of New South Wales.

Springbrook National Park

Only 34 km from Nerang, the Springbrook Plateau is the closest mountain to the Gold Coast. Springbrook National Park has three parts – **Springbrook Plateau** on the crest, **Mount Cougal** at the end of Currumbin Creek Road, and **Natural Bridge** just above the Numinbah Valley to the west.

At 900 m above sea level with an annual average rainfall of 3000 mm, the Springbrook Plateau is high and wet. On the road to the park and in the park itself are lookouts with views over the Gold Coast, Numinbah Valley and the Tweed Valley in New South Wales. The highlight of Springbrook is the 106-m **Purling Brook Falls**. A short walk from the picnic ground takes you to the top of the falls, while a 4-km return track descends to its base. **Natural Bridge** has a beautiful pool in a cavern into which a curtain of water cascades from a hole in the roof – a perfect place for a swim on a hot day. At night, the cave sparkles with glow worms.

Border Ranges Rugged ridges and deep valleys typify the ranges.

Natural Bridge is a waterfall that tumbles through a hole in the rock into an underground cavern in Springbrook National Park.

Mount Warning Volcano

The sharp peak of an almost-bare volcanic plug rears up 1157 m in the Tweed River Valley of northern New South Wales.

This is all that is left of a massive volcano that, 23 million years ago, was so high it had snow upon its crest. At that time it was active – spewing molten lava that streamed down its sides in all directions.

Today those long-cooled and solidified lava flows are the Lamington Plateau, Springbrook, Mount Tamborine and the rocky headlands along the southern Queensland coast.

Lamington National Park

Twenty thousand hectares is a lot of country by any measure, but when it is dense rainforest on mountain-tops up to 1100 m above sea level, plunging down deep impenetrable gorges and soaring to unscalable cliffs, you can experience wilderness on a grand scale. This is the **Lamington Plateau**, the emerald jewel of South-East Queensland, and all of it is preserved as the World-Heritage-listed Lamington National Park.

Although much of Lamington has been explored and opened for walkers, great swathes of its wildest terrain has never been traversed. The eastern and central parts of the park have extensive walking tracks, but the south-western half is untouched. The 160 km of walking tracks are split into two sections – Binna Burra and Green Mountains.

The **Binna Burra** section on the national park's north-eastern side is accessible from Brisbane via Canungra or Nerang, and from the Gold Coast via Nerang. A **Queensland Parks and Wildlife Service Information Centre** (Ph: 07 5533 3584, Mon to Fri 1 p.m. – 3.30 p.m.) is near the park boundary, 1.2 km before Binna Burra, where there is the privately run **Binna Burra Lodge and campground**, a picnic area and the main entrance to this section of the park's walking tracks.

The **Green Mountains** section is accessible by taking the winding, and often steep, 26-km road from Canungra to **O'Reilly's Rainforest Guesthouse**, located high in the middle of the park. Here, as well as the privately run guesthouse, are a QPWS information centre, a campground and a picnic area with entrances to walking tracks (Ph: 07 5544 0634, Mon, Wed, Thurs 9 a.m.–11 a.m. and Mon–Fri 1 p.m. – 3.30 p.m.).

O'Reilly's Rainforest Guesthouse

High in the rainforest, on a plot established by the O'Reilly family a century ago for farming, is O'Reilly's Rainforest Guesthouse, a popular resort offering week-long natural history theme programs and many spectacular walking tracks. Descendants of the original O'Reilly settlers still operate the mountain resort, which is the gateway to the Green Mountains section of the park.

One of the great walks of **Lamington National Park** is the track between O'Reilly's (Ph: 07 5544 0644) and **Binna Burra** (Ph: 07 5533 3622).

Right, top to bottom: **Enjoying the park** Camping, picnicking and wildlife watching along the rainforest tracks are just some of the activities to be enjoyed in Lamington National Park.

Binna Burra

On the north-east corner of Lamington National Park is Binna Burra, a resort lodge amidst the clouds.

The lodge is perched on a cliff-top where the land drops away steeply on three sides. On the third is the entrance to the spectacular walking tracks of the park.

Wildlife Along the Verges

Below, left to right: Whiptail Wallaby and joey; Australian Brush-turkey

One of the joys of driving through the countryside is catching a glimpse of native animals and birds in their natural habitat. A down side is that your car can be hazardous for unwary and unexpected wildlife. Fast-moving animals, such as kangaroos and wallabies, are particularly vulnerable and brush-turkeys often fall victim as they dart across the road at a pace that makes them difficult to see in time to avoid them. Lizards and snakes often bask on the roadway, absorbing warmth from the ground or lazing in the sun.

You can best experience the wildlife of the bush by stopping in a place where it is likely native animals and birds will be, switching off your car and sitting quietly, allowing the bush to come to life around you. Soon bird calls should resume, you may also hear the rustle of lizards in the undergrowth and kangaroos or wallabies may appear on the roadside verges to graze. In areas populated by Koalas, there is always the chance of spotting them asleep high in a gum tree.

Above, left to right: **Fungus growing up the trunk of a tree; Coomera Falls near Binna Burra** The Binna Burra section of Lamington National Park covers the north-eastern part of the park, above the Numinbah Valley, and has extensive walking trails.

Lamington National Park, Binna Burra Section

The Binna Burra section of Lamington National Park contains several walking tracks, some leading deep into the rainforest while others lead to lookouts offering spectacular views over the **Numinbah Valley** and the **Tweed River Valley** in New South Wales.

The **Border Track** runs southward through the rainforest past a stand of mossy Antarctic beech trees, relics of the last ice age. About 1.5 km in, the Coomera Circuit track winds to the right. Less than a kilometre further on, you can turn left on the Ships Stern and Daves Creek tracks. The Border track continues past **Joalah Lookout**, with a stunning view of Springbrook, and on to **Wagawn**, where a 200-m cliff-top lookout is level with the tip of Mount Warning, jutting out of the Tweed Valley. The Border Track then follows a dramatic path along the cliffs for several kilometres before turning north-westward to O'Reilly's. Binna Burra to Wagawn is a 20 km walk. Binna Burra to O'Reilly's is 23 km.

The **Coomera Circuit** is an 18 km track that meanders down the side of the **Coomera Gorge** to a spot where you can enjoy views of the **Coomera Falls**, which rush from a narrow crevice to plunge into a large pool. The track then leads up Coomera Creek, past several falls, to join the Border Track.

The 20-km **Ships Stern Track** can be travelled in either direction, but runs clockwise eastward from Binna Burra past several small waterfalls before dropping to Nixon Creek, where side tracks lead to **Ballunjui Falls**. The main track continues down the creek and then climbs to **Ships Stern**, a great bluff jutting out into the Numinbah Valley. It then follows the eastern side of Ships Stern southward through open heath before re-entering the rainforest to join the Border Track.

Wildlife Around Binna Burra

By day or night, the rainforest is alive with wildlife and places like the easily accessible forest at Binna Burra are ideal for wildlife watching. Spotlighting is one of the best ways to see the nocturnal inhabitants of the rainforest in their natural environment. Animals and birds not seen during the day – such as possums and owls – can often be seen at close quarters at night.

By day, as well as the prolific birdlife, many common reptiles and marsupials may be seen, including goannas, snakes, frogs (including the Green Tree-frog) and the Eastern Long-necked Turtle. Pademelons are seen regularly, particularly on grassy areas around the lodge in the evenings. Other animals found include Short-beaked Echidnas, quolls, Koalas and wallabies.

Rainforests and the eucalypt forests that fringe them are home to scores of birds – more than 120 species have been recorded in the Binna Burra area alone. Some species are elusive and patience is needed to spot them; others coexist happily with visitors and are easy to observe.

One of the most enthralling ways to experience the birdlife of the rainforest is to rise early and move quietly into the forest for the morning chorus. As nocturnal birds quieten with the approach of dawn, daytime birds begin to usher in the day with birdsong. Kookaburras are among the first to break the pre-dawn silence.

Above left: Mountain Possum with young. *Above right:* Spotlighting at Binna Burra. *Right:* Satin Bowerbird.

Lamington National Park, Green Mountains Section

The Green Mountains section's main walking track is the Border Track, towards the east, but there are several tracks leading off it before it reaches the cliff tops that overlook the Tweed River Valley. Westward from **O'Reilly's**, a track leads to the shimmering, misty curtain of **Morans Falls**.

The **Border Track** from O'Reilly's takes you up Canungra Creek to **Boolamoola Lookout** on the cliff-top near **Mount Bithongabel**; from there, you follow the cliffs around to **Wagawn** and on to **Binna Burra**. Tracks off the Border Track in the Green Mountains section include the **Valley of the Echoes Track** and the **Tooloona Track**. From O'Reilly's to Mount Bithongabel is 12.6 km.

The **Valley of the Echoes Track** runs in a 20.6-km circuit through the rugged country south of Mount Bithongabel and along the cliffs to **Echo Point**. From there it takes you down to the headwaters of the **Albert River**, through **Black Canyon**. The track passes several waterfalls and cascades before traversing high country to return to the Border Track along **Canungra Creek**.

Left to right: Chalahn Falls; Elizabeth Falls; Morans Falls Lamington National Park is blessed with many silvery, cascading waterfalls and the area around O'Reilly's Rainforest Guesthouse showcases some of the best of them.

Wildlife Around O'Reilly's

Below: Young Red-necked Pademelon

Being situated high in the middle of a rainforest, far from farms and towns, makes O'Reilly's a haven for animals, which live here in their natural habitat in harmony with humans and free from the dangers posed by domestic pets.

Among the 68 species of native animals in the area are kangaroos, pademelons, bandicoots, possums, Koalas, Platypus and the Common Planigale, a tiny but ferocious mouse-like carnivore.

World Famous O'Reilly's Birds

Above: Eastern Yellow Robin and chick

O'Reilly's is known internationally as one of Australia's premier birdwatching locations and more than 180 species have been recorded.

Regent and Satin Bowerbirds, Green Catbirds, Crimson Rosellas and Eastern Yellow Robins are among the many brightly coloured birds you may find here. In the deep rainforest is the elusive Albert's Lyrebird, the male of which makes a colourful display during the winter mating season.

The **Tooloona Track** follows **Tooloona Creek** through to the rocky **Tooloona Gorge** and passes more than a dozen falls along the way. At the gorge it meets the Border Track near **Wanungara Lookout**. From O'Reilly's to the point near Wanungara Lookout is an 18 km return walk.

The entrance to the **Morans Falls Track** is 1 km down the Canungra Road from O'Reilly's. The track is a 4.6 km return walk that descends through dense rainforest to the **Morans Falls Lookout** before leading you up above the falls.

Tree Top Walk

O'Reilly's Tree Top Walk takes you high into the rainforest canopy along a string of nine suspension bridges, most over 15 m above the ground. The 180 m walk leads to two observation decks (30 m above the ground) amid the twining branches of a strangler fig. Views out over the canopy are magnificent, but the Tree Top Walk also allows you to have a close-up view of the many orchids and ferns that nestle in forked branches or cling to tree trunks in the heights of the rainforest.

Tree Top Walk Suspended walkways high in the trees provide the perfect vantage point for you to experience the forest canopy and see the animals and birds that live off the fruits and flowers.

Great Walks of Queensland

The Queensland Parks and Wildlife Service has instituted six Great Walks that take bushwalkers through some of the State's most spectacular forests and national parks.

The walks use existing tracks through national parks, conservation areas, State forest and public and private land.

Gaps between existing tracks in each Great Walk are filled with new tracks and facilities to make the trek a unified hiking experience.

Top to bottom: **Fungus; Common Wombat; Barking Owl; Feathertail Gliders.**

Gold Coast Hinterland Great Walk

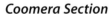

Trek through some of the most magnificent mountainous country in the State – the **Lamington Plateau, Numinbah Valley** and **Springbrook** in the **Border Ranges** – on one of the State's most spectacular walks. The walk, when completed, will combine existing tracks in national parks with new trails, creating a continuous walk that passes through rainforest mountains, open forest and valleys from the Green Mountains section of **Lamington National Park** to **Springbrook** overlooking the Gold Coast. Much of the walk will be through the world's largest subtropical rainforest remnant. As well as seeing the dense rainforest firsthand, in many places walkers will have spectacular views over **Mount Warning**, the **Tweed Valley** and the **Numinbah Valley**. Along the route are rainbow-lit waterfalls and clear mountain streams. Until the final route is completed, walkers can get a taste of the Great Walk by following the existing national park tracks, which are likely to be part of the finalised walk.

Lamington National Park Great Walk Section

Albert River Section

It is proposed that the walk will begin on the Border Track, near **O'Reilly's Rainforest Guesthouse**, high in the Green Mountains section of Lamington National Park. After 4 km, it will likely leave the Border Track and pass through forests of ancient moss-covered Antarctic beech to the **Albert River**, following the river past several waterfalls to the **Valley of the Echoes Lookout**. It then rejoins the Border Track along the escarpment of the **McPherson Range** before diverging to the Coomera Track. O'Reilly's to the Coomera Track turn-off is 17 km.

Coomera Section

This section is almost 17 km long and winds down to the Coomera River, passing cascades along the way to the **Coomera Lookout**, where you can take in views over the **Coomera Gorge** and **Coomera Falls**. The track rejoins the Border Track before backtracking 400 m to take you back along the Ships Stern Track.

Strangler fig These giants grow up and around a host tree, which eventually dies and rots away.

Misty moods Clouds shroud the dense rainforest, giving it a mystic ambience.

Mountain Inhabitants

Below left: Lamington Blue Cray. *Below right:* Platypus

The diverse environments encountered along the Gold Coast Hinterland Great Walk provide bushwalkers with the chance to see a variety of wildlife.

Keep an eye out for the colourful Lamington Blue Cray, which occupies streams high in the dense rainforest and is often seen crawling through the leaf litter when migrating between waterholes. Along the rainforest walking tracks, there is often the chance of catching a glimpse of snakes and lizards, while in the open forests you might see wallabies, pademelons and possums. If you are quiet, you may even happen across a Platypus in one of the cool, clear mountain streams.

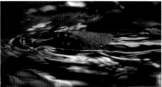

Ships Stern Section

On this section the walk will follow the existing Ships Stern Circuit to **Binna Burra**. The track winds its way past **Nagarigoon Falls** and the Nagarigoon campsite (once a forestry camp) then diverts to take you to the top of **Ballunjui Falls**, the main falls on Nixon Creek, which flows into the Numinbah Valley. Another route can be along the Daves Creek Circuit through open eucalypt forest and heath speckled with grass-trees and macrozamias. The track then follows the eastern escarpment of Ships Stern to the bluff's northern end, where it descends to Nixon Creek and follows the waterway through stands of piccabeen palms to the base of Ballunjui Falls. From here, you climb out of the Nixon Creek gorge and head on to Binna Burra. This section of the walk is about 12 km.

Numinbah–Springbrook Great Walk Section

When completed, the Gold Coast Hinterland Great Walk is expected to link the Lamington Section with Springbrook via new trails through the **Numinbah Valley**. This will allow walkers to continue from **Binna Burra** to Springbrook, following the paths in **Springbrook National Park**.

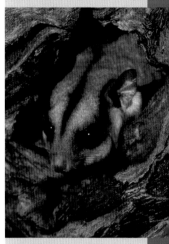

Sugar Gliders spend the daylight hours in a log-hollow nest, venturing out at night to feed.

Wildlife Encounters

Left: Spotted-tail Quolls are often seen in Lamington National Park.
Below right: Boyd's Rainforest Dragon.

Snakes and lizards are common in the depths of the rainforest, but seeing them is often difficult. They keenly sense human presence and often hide or depart well before you have a chance to observe them. To increase your chances of seeing reptiles, walk slowly and quietly through their likely habitat or sit and give them time to emerge to go about their life, allowing you to watch them in their natural surroundings.

Areas around streams and rock pools are good places to sit, wait and watch. As well as water dwellers – Platypus, crayfish, insects, frogs and turtles – birds, lizards, snakes, marsupial mice and animals such as the Spotted-tail Quoll might come into view and give an extra dimension to your rainforest experience.

Campsites along the Gold Coast Hinterland Great Walk

The Great Walks of Queensland are planned to allow walkers to cover many existing trails as a single trek over a number of days, stopping overnight at campsites or at commercial accommodation where it is available. Alternatively, walkers can start at accessible places along the walk and cover only chosen sections.

The Gold Coast Hinterland Great Walk is expected to have numerous overnight campsites, some of them existing, some to be built. Commercial overnight accommodation is already available at O'Reilly's, Binna Burra and on Springbrook. Walkers will be able to traverse a wonderfully unique, World-Heritage-listed part of Queensland, experiencing environments that a great variety of native animals and birds call home.

Look, Don't Touch

All plants and native animals in national parks are protected. Ensure that they remain unaffected by your presence by leaving natural places as pristine as you found them. Anything that you take in with you should be taken out with you when you leave.

Removing plants and animals from national parks and reserves is illegal.

Left to right: **Antarctic beech forest; Vine forest; Subtropical rainforest** The rainforest is a green world, often softened by cloud or mist. The thick canopy means only weak sunlight filters through to the floor, keeping the forest cool and damp.

Index

Acknowledgements

Photography: Steve Parish

Additional photography: Raoul Slater: pp. 8 & 77 Gympie Gold Mining Museum; John Oxley Library, State Library of Queensland 186091 & 177212: p. 8 Federation celebration, Queen St, 1901 & p. 10 Edward Street, Brisbane floods, 1974; Greg Harm: p. 13 Coolum Kite Festival & p. 21 Dragon Boats on the Brisbane River; Museum of Brisbane: p. 25 Exhibition space, Museum of Brisbane; Yaa Asantwaa Eleanor Adjei: p. 25 Main Auditorium, City Hall; Justine Walpole: p. 29 Performing Arts Centre; Sir Thomas Brisbane Planetarium: p. 37 Cosmic Skydome; Peter Slater: p. 42 Bell Miner, p. 80 Kingfisher, p. 83 Pacific Baza, p. 88 Suberb Fairy-wren; Ian Morris: p. 45, Peron's Tree-frog; courtesy of UnderWater World, Queensland's Largest Oceanarium & Aquarium: p. 67 Family with seal; Marcus Keys, courtesy of Jondaryan Woolshed Historical Museum & Park: p. 92 Jondaryan Woolshed; Len H. Smith: p. 95 Lyrebird; Geoff Rayner, courtesy of Stanthorpe Apple and Grape Harvest Festival: p. 97 Miss Southern Belle Float, Apple and Grape Festival; Aureo Martelli/APL: p. 98 Sphinx Rock, Girraween National Park; Sea World: p. 102 Polar Bears, p. 112 Dolphins; Dale Blackmore/APL: p. 105 Casey Mears driving, Honda Indy 300, 2001; Movie World: p. 112 Sylvester; Wet 'n' Wild: p. 112 Buccaneer Bay; Ripleys' Belive it or Not: p. 113 Ripleys' Belive it or Not.

Front cover, clockwise from top right: Humpback Whale; Brisbane; Pumicestone Passage; Gold Coast; Bunya Mountains; Chalahn Falls. Back cover, left to right: Point Lookout (and title page); Kangaroo Point. Inside front flap: Fraser Island. Inside back flap: Steve Parish; Rainbow Lorikeet.

Text: Bob Johnson, Peter Fox & Karin Cox

Series designed: Leanne Nobilio

Finished art: Leanne Nobilio, Catherine Prentice, Fanne Kosztolanyi

Editorial: Wynne Webber; Michele Perry & Karin Cox, SPP

Publisher: Donald Greig

Published by Steve Parish Publishing Pty Ltd
PO Box 1058, Archerfield, Queensland 4108 Australia

www.steveparish.com.au

© copyright Steve Parish Publishing Pty Ltd

ISBN 174021745 4
10 9 8 7 6 5 4 3 2 1

FOR PRODUCTS
www.steveparish.com.au

FOR LIMITED EDITION PRINTS
www.steveparishexhibits.com.au

FOR PHOTOGRAPHY EZINE
www.photographaustralia.com.au